The Amazing Adventures of
MR. GRANT MONEY

STRIVE press

Dear Reader,

Thank you for embarking on this exciting journey with "The Amazing Adventures of Mr. Grant Money." I'm thrilled to share with you the valuable insights and lessons contained within these pages, lessons that have empowered countless individuals and organizations to achieve remarkable success in their grant acquisition endeavors.

Grant funding is a powerful tool, and this book is designed to be your companion as you navigate the intricate world of grant writing. Within these stories lie not just narratives but essential lessons that will guide you toward securing funding for your projects. As you read and engage with the exercises, I hope you find inspiration and actionable strategies to elevate your grant acquisition efforts to new heights.

Throughout my career, I've had the privilege of assisting many individuals starting from ground zero, witnessing their transformation into successful grant seekers. The stories and lessons in this book encapsulate some of the crucial insights that have contributed to their achievements.

However, I must take a moment to introduce you to another invaluable resource—the "Grant Writing That Gets Funded" training. This training has been a cornerstone in the success stories of numerous students and organizations. Tailored for beginners and intermediate grant professionals, it offers clear and comprehensive guidance. Participants not only absorb my exclusive Grant Writing Success Formula but also leave with a personalized 30-Day Grant Empowerment Strategy and Grant Readiness Resource.

Our training has played a pivotal role in agencies securing substantial funding, ranging from $25,000 to millions, in a remarkably short period. You can witness some of these success stories at WowTheyDidIt.com. I am confident that with our support, you could be the next success story, unlocking a bountiful windfall of grant funding for your endeavors.

Imagine the impact on your team as they gain insights, adopt best practices, and leverage industry secrets, giving your agency a competitive edge. This training could be the pivotal factor that distinguishes you from others, ensuring you secure the grants you pursue.

As Kjeld Linstead, a past participant, expressed, "Thanks again for the grants class a few months ago... Since taking your class, I have landed nearly $4 Million in state and federal grants for the City of Redlands."

For more information about the Grant Writing That Gets Funded training, please visit GrantWritingClasses.org. You can also secure your spot by calling 1-888-293-0284. This investment in your organization's financial stability is a strategic move towards a more prosperous future.

Best Regards,

Rodney
Grant Central USA

P.S. Be sure to try our free grant training at StrategicGrantWriting.com.

The Amazing Adventures of
MR. GRANT MONEY

The Artful Navigator: Mr. Grant Money's Chronicles

VOLUME TWO

RODNEY WALKER

STRIVE press

For related titles and support materials, visit our online catalog at www.mrgrantmoney.com and www.grantcentralusa.com

Chief Editor: Laine Minerales
Editorial Assistant: Daniel Tuano
Production Supervisor: Joerje Galo
Electronic Composition: Jairus Agoncillo
Photographer: Studio 5404
Executive Marketing Manager: Jimmy Moore

Discover the breadth of our series, encompassing a myriad of crucial topics. Delve into the realms of grant acquisition, college scholarships, entrepreneurship, social impact, philanthropy, and beyond. Unearth a treasure trove of knowledge and empowerment within our diverse collection. Explore the wealth of insights awaiting you across these transformative series.

To inquire about utilizing The Amazing Adventures of Mr. Grant Money books in the classroom, securing licensing, and exploring special pricing for bulk orders, kindly contact us at info@grantcentralusa.com.

ISBN: 978-0-9659275-2-9

Printed in the United States

Dedication

To my dearest father, Fred Walker Jr.,
Your unwavering support, wisdom, and love have been my guiding stars throughout my life. This book is dedicated to you, as a token of my deepest gratitude for all that you've done. Your strength and resilience continue to inspire me every day.

With love and appreciation,
Rodney

PREFACE

The Adventures of Mr. Grant Money: A Journey of Transformation

In the world of grant acquisition, where dreams take flight on the wings of well-crafted proposals, where passion meets purpose, and where communities are transformed through the power of giving, I invite you to embark on a remarkable journey. These adventures are not just a recounting of tales but a testament to the evolution of a grant professional who started with the humblest of beginnings and emerged as a Master Grant Acquisition Specialist.

Over two decades in the making, these stories are a blend of my real-life experiences as a grant professional. They unfold the lessons learned, the challenges faced, and the victories achieved. From the time when I was a novice, wide-eyed and eager to write my first grant proposal, seeking a mere $25,000 for a youth development program, to the present, where I've had the privilege of assisting thousands of individuals and organizations worldwide each year, this journey is one of profound transformation.

It all began with the idea of sharing inspiring tales through a series of blog posts, offering snippets of wisdom and knowledge to those in the world of grants. Yet, as I put pen to paper, these stories took on a life of their own, weaving together to form something magical, something special. What started as a caterpillar of inspiration morphed into a butterfly waiting for you to leap onto its wings and embark on a series of captivating journeys.

This collection is intended to educate and entertain, to offer fresh ideas and insights for seasoned veterans of the grant profession, to guide and inspire newcomers, and perhaps even awaken the curiosity of a young student unaware of the incredible world of grant acquisition.

In this adventure, we'll dive into the core of grant writing, explore the depths of fundraising, and unearth the hidden treasures of effective philanthropy. We'll laugh, we'll learn, and we'll leap beyond the boundaries of the ordinary.

But at the heart of it all, this is a testament to the power of belief. For, as you'll discover, belief is the force that propels dreams into reality. As you journey through these tales, remember one word: BELIEVE!

Now, dear reader, join me as we venture forth into the world of Mr. Grant Money's adventures. Let's explore, learn, and transform together. The journey begins with a single page, and the possibilities are endless.

TABLE OF CONTENT

Introduction   8

The Grant Whisperer: Mr. Grant Money's Insightful Consultation   9

The Divine Art of Grant Acquisition: Mr. Grant Money's Miracle at the Museum   16

Driven by Excellence: Mr. Grant Money's Precision Lifestyle   22

The Grant Maestro's Grand Reveal: Secrets of $65 Million Success   28

Taking the Leap: Mr. Grant Money's Airborne Epiphany   34

Rhythms of Impact: Mr. Grant Money's Journey to Empowerment   40

Grant Money's Upward Bound: Soaring with Balloons in Albuquerque   46

The Alamo Epiphany: Mr. Grant Money's Insights on Grant Acquisition   52

Grant Acquisition Unleashed: Mr. Grant Money's Art of Winning   58

Brushstrokes of Wisdom: Mr. Grant Money's Artistic Adventure   64

Afterward   70

About the Author   71

Boost Your Grant Game: Additional Resources   72

INTRODUCTION

Welcome back to the enthralling world of philanthropy, grants, and remarkable exploits as we rejoin the dashing Mr. Grant Money on his captivating journey. In this second volume, "The Artful Navigator," prepare yourself for another collection of gripping stories, each laden with lessons and insights that will revolutionize your approach to grant acquisition.

As you delve into the ten riveting stories, you'll traverse diverse landscapes, from art museums to the skies of Albuquerque, and from whispered insights to artistic epiphanies. Each story will draw you into its unique realm, transporting you to different corners of the grant acquisition universe, where you'll meet captivating characters, explore the intricacies of grantsmanship, and discover invaluable secrets to success.

Following each of these engaging tales, you'll encounter exercises tailor-made to guide you in implementing the strategies employed by the enigmatic Mr. Grant Money himself. These exercises are designed not just to teach you about grant acquisition but to empower you to harness the principles shared in these stories and apply them to your own grant-seeking endeavors.

Moreover, discussions and questions will encourage you to reflect on the narratives, extracting deeper meanings and understanding that could shape your grant acquisition approach. Powerful quotes and one standout "BIG Idea" from each story will serve as touchstones for your journey, ensuring that you leave no lesson unlearned. But that's not all; in every story, you'll also find an entertaining word search puzzle built around the central lesson. It's a unique twist that adds an element of fun while reinforcing the key takeaways.

This book is designed for a diverse readership, including grant writing instructors, students venturing into the world of grants, new grant writers, experienced grant professionals, fundraisers, grant consultants, nonprofit organizations, executive directors, government agencies, faith-based organizations, and anyone who seeks to excel in the domain of grant acquisition.

It's essential to understand what this book is and what it is not. "The Artful Navigator" is not a step-by-step guide on how to write a grant proposal, nor is it a dry account of the mechanics of grant writing. Rather, it's an immersive adventure, narrated through the experiences of the enigmatic Mr. Grant Money. It will spark your imagination, inspire creativity, and challenge the way you think about grant acquisition. Through its stories, exercises, and discussions, it will empower you to approach grantsmanship with a renewed sense of purpose and vision.

So, as we embark on another thrilling expedition with Mr. Grant Money, remember to keep an open mind and an eager heart. The journey that awaits you is one of transformation and growth. Let these stories and exercises illuminate your path, and may your own grant acquisition endeavors be forever elevated. Get ready to navigate the artful world of grants with confidence and style, and uncover the boundless opportunities that lie ahead.

THE GRANT WHISPERER

The Amazing Adventures of
MR GRANT MONEY

The Grant Whisperer: Mr. Grant Money's Insightful Consultation

*From Meticulous Grants to Unmasking Reputation Woes
– His Impact Unveiled*

Mr. Grant Money, with his unparalleled attention to detail, effortless style, and intelligence, continued his journey of helping charities and government agencies secure the funding they needed. He had always believed that "the Dollar is in the Details," and it was this meticulous approach that set him apart from most consultants.

One day, a top-notch executive director from a large nonprofit in the Baltimore area approached Mr. Grant Money's trusted assistant, pleading for an exception to the customary $5,000 deposit required to be placed on Mr. Grant Money's one-year waiting list. The executive's cause struck a chord with Mr. Grant Money, as it focused on addressing cancer in children—a cause that was deeply personal to him, as he had lost his beloved mother to the disease and cherished her memory.

Sensitivity to the charity's cause prompted Mr. Grant Money to agree to a 30-minute meeting with the executive, Tom Ellis, in the plush executive lounge of the airport for a small fee of $2,500. As they sat in a private room, Mr. Grant Money listened attentively to Tom's plea for consideration.

After just a few minutes of discussion, Mr. Grant Money's piercing eyes looked directly into Tom's, and he discerned the root problem plaguing the executive and his organization. In his usual astute manner, Mr. Grant Money calmly stated, "Your organization has a reputation problem that you've allowed to go unchecked."

Tom was taken aback by the directness of Mr. Grant Money's diagnosis. It was clear that Mr. Grant Money saw right through to the heart of the issue. Intrigued and eager to understand how Mr. Grant Money could help, Tom asked, "What can we do to address this reputation problem?"

Mr. Grant Money posed two penetrating questions to gauge whether the organization was a good fit for his expertise. "Are you willing to invest in a comprehensive reputation management strategy, and are you committed to making the necessary changes within your organization to rebuild trust and credibility?"

Tom responded without hesitation, "Yes, we are willing to invest, and we are committed to making the necessary changes."

With a knowing nod, Mr. Grant Money promptly ended the meeting. "I shall see," he said with a hint of intrigue, leaving Tom with a sense of hope and determination.

As Mr. Grant Money's driver whisked him away to a private fundraiser in Washington, D.C., he couldn't help but reflect on the power of his work. He was indeed solving the world's problems one grant at a time. Whether through securing funding or diagnosing deeper issues within organizations, Mr. Grant Money's journey continued, leaving a trail of transformation and positive change in his wake.

"In the world of grants, it's the meticulous attention to detail that reveals the Dollar's true hiding place. My secret?
The Dollar is in the Details."

-Mr.Grant Money

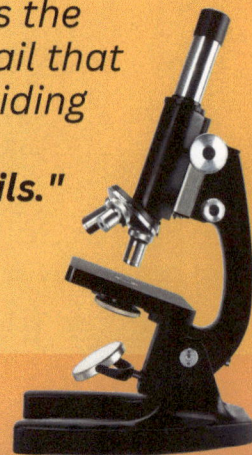

Exercise: "The Reputation Diagnosis and Revitalization Plan"

Mr. Grant Money's insight into the reputation issues faced by the nonprofit organization in the story highlights the importance of addressing reputation problems proactively. This exercise encourages individuals or teams to diagnose and develop a plan to revitalize an organization's reputation.

Objective: To learn how to identify reputation issues and develop a strategic plan to rebuild trust and credibility for an organization.

Steps:

1. Evaluate Your Organization's Reputation:
- Reflect on your organization's current reputation and any concerns or issues that may be affecting it. Consider internal and external factors, such as public perception, media coverage, past incidents, or trust issues.

2. Form a Reputation Diagnosis Team:
- Assemble a team within your organization or collaborate with key stakeholders who can help assess and diagnose reputation-related problems. Include individuals with diverse perspectives and expertise.

3. Conduct a Reputation Audit:
- Begin a comprehensive reputation audit by examining public perception, feedback from stakeholders, online reviews, and any available data. Identify areas where the organization's reputation may be compromised.

4. Identify Root Problems:
- Work with your reputation diagnosis team to identify the underlying causes of reputation issues. Is it a specific incident, a lack of transparency, miscommunication, or other factors that have contributed to a negative reputation?

5. Set Clear Reputation Goals:
- Define what you want to achieve regarding your organization's reputation. Establish clear and measurable goals, such as rebuilding trust, enhancing credibility, or improving public perception.

6. Create a Reputation Revitalization Plan:
- Develop a strategic plan that outlines specific actions and initiatives to address the identified reputation problems. Consider measures such as transparency improvements, community engagement, crisis management, or communication strategies.

7. Allocate Resources and Responsibilities:
- Determine the resources needed to execute the revitalization plan, including personnel, budgets, and time. Assign responsibilities to team members and stakeholders involved in the process.

8. Implementation of the Plan:
- Begin implementing the reputation revitalization plan, focusing on the most urgent and impactful actions first. Monitor progress and make necessary adjustments as the plan unfolds.

9. Communicate Transparently:
- Be open and transparent in your communication with stakeholders, acknowledging the reputation issues and your commitment to resolving them. Share progress and changes made to rebuild trust.

10. Seek External Expertise if Needed:
- If the reputation issues are complex or require specialized knowledge, consider consulting with external experts, such as reputation management professionals or public relations specialists.

11. Evaluate Progress and Adjust:

- Regularly evaluate the progress of your reputation revitalization plan. Use metrics, feedback, and data to measure the impact of your efforts. Adjust the plan as needed based on the results.

12. Celebrate Achievements:

- Acknowledge and celebrate the milestones and improvements achieved in rebuilding your organization's reputation. Share the successes with your stakeholders to reinforce trust and confidence.

By engaging in this exercise, individuals or teams can address reputation issues within their organizations, just as Mr. Grant Money's insight helped the nonprofit organization begin the journey of revitalizing its reputation. Rebuilding trust and credibility is a valuable step toward achieving your organization's mission and goals.

"To solve the world's problems, we must first diagnose the root issues plaguing organizations and have the courage to address them. It's not just about securing grants, it's about transforming from within."
- Mr. Grant Money

Discussion Questions

1. Mr. Grant Money's direct diagnosis of the nonprofit's reputation problem played a crucial role in their conversation. How significant is honest and candid feedback in addressing organizational challenges, particularly in the context of grant acquisition and fundraising? How can nonprofits and government agencies effectively address reputation issues to regain trust and credibility?

2. The story highlights the personal connection between Mr. Grant Money and the nonprofit's cause, which centered on childhood cancer. To what extent should personal experiences and passions influence grant acquisition strategies and decisions? How might an individual's personal connection to a cause impact their approach and effectiveness in securing grants?

3. Mr. Grant Money posed two key questions to gauge the nonprofit's readiness for his expertise: their willingness to invest in a reputation management strategy and their commitment to making necessary organizational changes. How important is the willingness to invest time, effort, and resources in grant acquisition success? What role does organizational readiness and adaptability play in the success of grant acquisition strategies?

4. The story suggests that Mr. Grant Money's approach to problem-solving extends beyond grant acquisition to diagnosing deeper organizational issues. What are some common organizational challenges that can impact grant acquisition efforts, and how can consultants like Mr. Grant Money assist nonprofits and government agencies in addressing these challenges?

5. The story mentions Mr. Grant Money's commitment to solving the world's problems one grant at a time. What is the broader impact of successful grant acquisition on communities and society? How do grant acquisition specialists like Mr. Grant Money contribute to positive change and transformation at a larger scale?

💡 **Big Idea** "The Reputation Doctor Consultation Service"

Taking inspiration from Mr. Grant Money's approach to identifying and addressing reputation issues, launch a unique "Reputation Doctor" consultation service. This service would specialize in diagnosing and prescribing solutions for reputation problems. Just like Mr. Grant Money's unique approach to grant consultation, the "Reputation Doctor" consultants would offer insights, advice, and action plans to individuals and organizations seeking to improve their public image. This creative and specialized consultancy could potentially fill a niche market for those looking to rebuild trust and credibility in today's digital age.

🔍 Word Search

Join the world of grant acquisition with Mr. Grant Money and explore the meticulous details that set him apart. As he helps charities and government agencies secure vital funding, you'll find the Dollar is truly in the Details.

In this puzzle, discover the words related to the extraordinary adventures of Mr. Grant Money. Can you find all the hidden words that capture the essence of this remarkable story?

Now, here are the 14 words for the word search puzzle based on the story:

L	C	T	S	E	I	T	I	R	A	H	C	E	E
G	O	R	L	M	A	N	A	G	E	M	E	N	T
T	N	E	M	N	R	E	V	O	G	V	N	T	R
A	S	C	E	A	T	G	M	N	E	C	E	D	T
A	U	B	A	L	T	I	M	O	R	E	R	E	S
S	L	A	R	I	A	N	E	O	N	T	D	T	O
S	T	E	C	A	N	C	E	R	D	C	L	A	I
F	A	C	A	T	T	I	E	T	U	H	I	I	G
U	N	A	A	M	C	A	S	M	T	O	H	L	D
N	T	E	M	O	T	H	E	R	O	T	C	S	C
D	S	I	S	E	N	S	I	T	I	V	I	T	Y
I	U	I	I	T	M	E	E	T	I	N	G	M	U
N	N	O	I	T	A	T	U	P	E	R	N	A	T
G	M	R	G	R	A	N	T	M	O	N	E	Y	I

BALTIMORE
DETAILS
CHILDREN
SENSITIVITY
GOVERNMENT
CHARITIES
FUNDING
MANAGEMENT
MEETING
REPUTATION
CANCER
MOTHER
MRGRANTMONEY
CONSULTANT

"Mr. Grant Money's astute diagnosis of the organization's reputation problem exemplifies the power of discernment and the willingness to confront challenges head-on. His approach offers valuable insights into tackling the deeper issues that can affect an organization's success."

THE DIVINE ART OF GRANT ACQUISITION

The Divine Art of Grant Acquisition: Mr. Grant Money's Miracle at the Museum

How One Man Transformed a Museum's Fate and Unlocked $13.5 Million

In the realm of grant acquisition, Mr. Grant Money seemed to possess a touch of the divine. His ability to accomplish great feats with an ease and effortlessness left many of his clients in awe. To them, the speed and success with which he operated bordered on the mysterious and godlike.

One notable instance took place with a world-renowned museum that had set its sights on a monumental funding goal of $13.5 million. The museum had previously engaged a team of consultants to help them secure the necessary funds, but despite their best efforts, success remained elusive.

Enter Mr. Grant Money.

With a keen eye and a methodical approach, he reviewed the previous consulting team's strategy and identified three major issues that had been overlooked, deemed as minor nuisances by the prior consultants. To Mr. Grant Money, these were like three pillars holding up a shaky structure, and he knew they needed to be addressed immediately.

The first issue was a lack of specificity in the museum's grant proposals. Mr. Grant Money saw that they were missing the mark by not tailoring their requests to the unique interests and priorities of potential funders. He worked with the team to develop highly targeted proposals that spoke directly to the passions of potential supporters.

The second issue was a breakdown in communication between the museum's leadership and the consulting team. Mr. Grant Money recognized the importance of a unified front and established regular meetings to ensure everyone was on the same page. This eliminated confusion and created a cohesive vision for the grant-seeking process.

The third issue was a failure to track and document the progress of grant applications. Mr. Grant Money knew that every interaction with potential funders was an opportunity to learn and improve. He implemented a robust tracking system that allowed the museum to evaluate their successes and refine their approach based on real-time feedback.

As weeks turned into months, Mr. Grant Money orchestrated a series of seemingly small marginal victories. Each successful grant application, each positive interaction with a potential funder, contributed to a growing momentum that was palpable within the museum's team.

And then, as if by some preordained design, the museum received news that they had been awarded a grant of $13.5 million. It was the culmination of Mr. Grant Money's meticulous attention to detail, his ability to see through the errors of the previous approach, and his talent for transforming seemingly small victories into a monumental win.

With a confidence that bordered on the supernatural, Mr. Grant Money placed his hat on his head and picked up his walking stick. He smiled, leaving no doubt that he had once again worked his magic. As he walked out the door, he knew that his next adventure awaited, and there were countless more grants to be won and communities to be uplifted.

Exercise: "The Power of Meticulous Grant Acquisition Strategy"

This exercise is designed to help individuals or teams develop a meticulous grant acquisition strategy inspired by Mr. Grant Money's approach in the story.

Objective: To create a comprehensive and detail-oriented grant acquisition strategy that increases the chances of securing grants.

Steps:

1. Identify Grant Goals:
- Clearly define your grant acquisition goals. What funding do you need, and for what purpose? Write down your specific objectives.

2. Review Past Grant Proposals (Issue 1 - Specificity):
- If applicable, review any past grant proposals and assess whether they lacked specificity or tailoring to potential funders' interests. Identify areas for improvement.

3. Create a Targeted Proposal Template:
- Develop a template for grant proposals that can be tailored to the unique interests and priorities of potential funders. Include sections that can be customized for each application.

4. Communication Plan (Issue 2 - Communication Breakdown):
- Address any potential communication breakdowns within your organization. Define roles and responsibilities for those involved in the grant-seeking process. Establish regular meetings to ensure everyone is aligned.

5. Implement a Tracking System (Issue 3 - Progress Tracking):
- Create a comprehensive tracking system to document the progress of grant applications. Use spreadsheets or project management software to monitor deadlines, interactions, and application statuses.

6. Research Potential Funders:
- Conduct in-depth research to identify potential grant opportunities and funders whose missions align with your organization's goals. Develop a list of prospective funders.

7. Develop a Comprehensive Calendar:
- Create a grant application calendar that outlines application deadlines, requirements, and submission dates for each prospective funder. Ensure your team is aware of key dates.

8. Tailor Proposals for Each Funder:
- Customize grant proposals for each funder, ensuring that your applications speak directly to their passions and priorities. Use the template created earlier to streamline the process.

9. Engage in Relationship Building:
- Establish and nurture relationships with potential funders. Attend networking events or reach out to funders directly to introduce your organization and its mission.

10. Regular Progress Evaluation:
- Periodically review the progress of your grant acquisition strategy. Assess the effectiveness of your tailored proposals, communication plan, and tracking system. Make adjustments as needed.

11. Maintain a Knowledge Repository:
- Create a repository of successful grant proposals, templates, and best practices. Use this knowledge repository as a resource for future applications.

12. Celebration and Feedback:
- Celebrate each grant secured as a small victory, and use these successes to build momentum. Encourage team members to provide feedback and share lessons learned for continuous improvement.

By following this exercise, you can develop a meticulous grant acquisition strategy that addresses the three key issues identified in Mr. Grant Money's approach. This strategy will help increase your organization's chances of securing grants by tailoring proposals, improving communication, and implementing effective tracking and feedback mechanisms.

Discussion Questions

1. In this story, Mr. Grant Money identified and addressed three key issues that the previous consulting team had overlooked. How crucial is the ability to diagnose and remedy such issues in the grant acquisition process, and what challenges might organizations face in recognizing and addressing these issues?

2. Mr. Grant Money's approach emphasized tailoring grant proposals to the unique interests of potential funders. How significant is personalized and targeted messaging in the grant acquisition process? What strategies and practices can organizations adopt to ensure their proposals resonate with potential donors?

3. Effective communication and unity within the organization were key areas of focus for Mr. Grant Money. How can improved communication and a shared vision positively impact grant acquisition efforts? What are some common challenges that organizations encounter in maintaining alignment between their leadership and consulting teams?

4. The story emphasizes the importance of tracking and documenting progress in the grant application process. How can tracking systems enhance the effectiveness of grant acquisition efforts? What role does continuous feedback and evaluation play in refining grant application strategies?

5. The story portrays Mr. Grant Money's work as having a seemingly miraculous or divine touch. What attributes or qualities are vital in a successful grant acquisition specialist, and how can individuals or organizations seeking grants benefit from such expertise? How does the work of a grant acquisition specialist impact communities and organizations?

💡 Big Idea "Develop a Grant Application Tracking Software"

Emulate Mr. Grant Money's commitment to tracking and monitoring the progress of grant applications by creating a specialized grant application tracking software. Design a user-friendly platform that allows nonprofit organizations and grant seekers to manage their grant proposals systematically. Features could include proposal customization, automated communication alerts, and real-time feedback integration, helping users optimize their grant applications effectively.

🔍 Word Search

Prepare to dive into the world of grant acquisition with Mr. Grant Money, a figure who seems to possess an almost divine touch when it comes to securing funds. As we explore his legendary feats in grant acquisition, search for the hidden words related to his remarkable journey in the puzzle below.

In this puzzle, discover the words related to the extraordinary adventures of Mr. Grant Money. Can you find all the hidden words that capture the essence of this remarkable story?

Now, here are the 14 words for the word search puzzle based on the story:

C	U	M	R	S	S	U	C	C	E	S	S	C	R
C	E	A	S	T	N	A	T	L	U	S	N	O	C
O	S	R	V	E	L	S	N	E	E	A	C	P	E
M	U	G	S	P	E	C	I	F	I	C	I	T	Y
M	P	I	S	R	A	T	D	M	S	C	Y	S	G
U	E	N	E	I	D	I	I	S	U	G	G	N	I
N	R	A	I	M	E	I	V	T	I	E	E	E	I
I	N	L	R	P	R	L	I	R	L	L	S	A	N
C	A	I	O	I	S	C	N	A	R	I	I	U	E
A	T	I	T	L	H	K	E	T	O	N	N	D	M
T	U	A	C	L	I	L	M	E	S	C	C	I	U
I	R	C	I	A	P	R	O	G	R	E	S	S	E
O	A	G	V	R	C	P	N	Y	I	R	L	S	T
N	L	C	N	S	U	T	R	A	C	K	I	N	G

SPECIFICITY
STRATEGY
VICTORIES
SUPERNATURAL
TRACKING
MARGINAL
COMMUNICATION
LEADERSHIP
PILLARS
MUSEUM
SUCCESS
DIVINE
PROGRESS
CONSULTANTS

"Mr. Grant Money's remarkable ability to diagnose and rectify overlooked issues in the grant acquisition process is a testament to the power of methodical problem-solving. His approach turns challenges into opportunities, proving that success often hinges on addressing the small details."

DRIVEN BY EXCELLENCE

Driven by Excellence: Mr. Grant Money's Precision Lifestyle

When Fast Cars, Fine Dining, and Grant Success Intersect

Mr. Grant Money's adventures in the world of grant acquisition were not his only passions. He had a love for the finer things in life, including expensive and fast cars, exquisite cuisine, and the highest standards of excellence for himself, his team, and his clients.

One sunny afternoon in Los Angeles, Mr. Grant Money found himself at an exclusive charity event held at a luxury car showroom. The event was a fundraiser for a nonprofit dedicated to improving education in underserved communities. As he mingled with the guests, his keen eye couldn't help but notice the sleek, high-performance sports cars on display.

His attention was particularly drawn to a limited-edition, handcrafted Italian sports car—one that had been customized to perfection. Mr. Grant Money couldn't resist the allure of the automobile, and he found himself in a deep conversation with the showroom's owner.

As they discussed the car's intricate details, Mr. Grant Money's meticulous attention to detail shone through. He asked about the engine specifications, the craftsmanship of the interior, and the precision of the vehicle's handling. It was clear that he appreciated excellence in all forms, whether it was in the world of grants or the world of automotive engineering.

The showroom owner, intrigued by Mr. Grant Money's passion and knowledge, extended an invitation for a private test drive. With a smile and a nod, Mr. Grant Money accepted, relishing the opportunity to experience the thrill of a high-performance machine.

As he sat behind the wheel, the engine roared to life, and Mr. Grant Money felt the power and precision of the finely-tuned masterpiece. The exhilarating ride through the winding streets of Los Angeles left him with a sense of exhilaration and a newfound appreciation for the craftsmanship of such vehicles.

But Mr. Grant Money's love for excellence didn't end with cars. It extended to his culinary preferences as well. He was known for his discerning palate and often sought out the finest restaurants in every city he visited. His team had learned to expect nothing less than perfection, just as he expected excellence from them in their grant acquisition endeavors.

When it came to his clients, Mr. Grant Money held them to the highest standards as well. He believed that success in grant acquisition required unwavering dedication, attention to detail, and a commitment to excellence. His clients knew that when they worked with him, they were embarking on a journey that demanded nothing less than their very best.

As the sun set over Los Angeles, Mr. Grant Money returned the sports car to the showroom, his appetite for excellence sated, at least for the moment. With a sense of satisfaction, he made his way to a renowned restaurant to savor a culinary masterpiece that rivaled the perfection he demanded in all aspects of his life.

With each new adventure, Mr. Grant Money continued to bring his meticulous attention to detail, his love for the finer things, and his unwavering commitment to excellence to the world of grant acquisition. It was a journey marked by high standards and a relentless pursuit of success, and it was a journey that showed no signs of slowing down.

Exercise: "Pursuing Excellence in Grant Acquisition"

In this exercise, you will reflect on Mr. Grant Money's pursuit of excellence and apply principles from his lifestyle to your grant acquisition efforts. By focusing on attention to detail, high standards, and commitment to excellence, you can improve your grant-seeking process and increase your chances of success.

Objective: To develop a commitment to excellence in grant acquisition by embracing attention to detail, high standards, and a passion for excellence.

Steps:

1. Set Clear Grant Acquisition Goals:
- Define your grant acquisition goals and the specific outcomes you wish to achieve. Clarity in your objectives is the first step toward excellence.

2. Attention to Detail:
- Examine your past grant applications and grant-seeking processes. Identify areas where attention to detail could have made a difference. Make a list of specific details to focus on in future applications.

3. High Standards in Proposal Crafting:
- Elevate the quality of your grant proposals. Research and incorporate best practices in proposal writing. Review examples of successful grant proposals to understand what high standards entail.

4. Excellence in Research:
- Improve your research process by identifying potential funders, their interests, and requirements. Create a comprehensive list of prospects and align your proposals with their priorities.

5. Feedback and Peer Review:
- Seek feedback from colleagues, mentors, or peers in the grant acquisition field. Encourage them to review your proposals and provide constructive criticism to help you refine your work.

6. Regularly Update Your Skills:

- Stay current with the latest trends and developments in grant acquisition. Attend workshops, webinars, and training sessions to refine your skills.

7. Commitment to Excellence in Execution:

- Embrace a commitment to excellence in all aspects of grant acquisition, from the initial research to proposal submission. Hold yourself and your team to high standards throughout the process.

8. Mentorship and Knowledge Sharing:

- If you have expertise in grant acquisition, consider mentoring others who are new to the field. Share your knowledge and encourage a culture of excellence among colleagues.

9. Monitoring and Continuous Improvement:

- After each grant submission, conduct a post-submission review. Analyze what went well and what could be improved. Use this feedback to continually enhance your grant acquisition process.

10. Celebrate Small Wins:

- Acknowledge and celebrate even the smallest achievements in your grant acquisition journey. Cultivate a culture of recognizing and appreciating excellence.

11. Commit to Excellence in All Aspects of Life:

- Just as Mr. Grant Money pursued excellence in his love for fine cars and exquisite dining, make a commitment to excellence in all areas of your life. The pursuit of excellence is a holistic endeavor.

By following this exercise, you will infuse a commitment to excellence into your grant acquisition efforts. Whether it's the meticulous crafting of proposals, attention to detail in research, or setting high standards in execution, the pursuit of excellence can significantly enhance your chances of success in securing grants.

Discussion Questions

1. Mr. Grant Money is depicted as a perfectionist with a strong focus on excellence, whether in the world of grant acquisition, fast cars, or fine dining. How do these characteristics shape his approach to grant acquisition, and what impact does his pursuit of excellence have on his clients and team?

2. The story portrays Mr. Grant Money's love for high-performance sports cars and his appreciation for craftsmanship. How might his passion for cars and attention to detail in the automotive world parallel his meticulous approach to grant acquisition? What lessons can be drawn from his focus on craftsmanship and precision?

3. Mr. Grant Money's discerning palate and search for the finest restaurants demonstrate his commitment to excellence in culinary experiences. How can this commitment to quality in one area of life reflect or influence his expectations for clients and colleagues in grant acquisition? What can organizations learn from his pursuit of perfection in different aspects of life?

4. The story suggests that Mr. Grant Money's clients are held to the highest standards and that he demands unwavering dedication and attention to detail. How can a commitment to excellence influence an organization's ability to secure grants and achieve its goals? What challenges and opportunities might organizations encounter when striving for such high standards?

5. Mr. Grant Money's unwavering commitment to excellence is described as a driving force in his life. How can individuals or organizations seeking grants incorporate a similar commitment to excellence into their grant acquisition strategies and approaches? What benefits and challenges might arise from this pursuit of perfection in the grant acquisition process?

💡 Big Idea "The Urban Grant Excellence Workshop"

Take inspiration from Mr. Grant Money's keynote address and create a practical Urban Grant Excellence Workshop for government officials, city planners, and grant-seeking professionals. This workshop would provide hands-on training on the key success factors highlighted in Mr. Grant Money's speech: strategic alignment, data-driven approaches, community engagement, collaborative partnerships, and robust grant management. By offering practical guidance and actionable strategies, participants would be better equipped to secure grants for urban development and community improvement projects.

🔍 Word Search

Get ready to dive into the world of Mr. Grant Money, a man of unparalleled excellence who combines his love for the finer things in life with his passion for grant acquisition. In this word search puzzle, discover 15 words that capture the essence of Mr. Grant Money's unwavering commitment to excellence in all he does.

In this puzzle, discover the words related to the extraordinary adventures of Mr. Grant Money. Can you find all the hidden words that capture the essence of this remarkable story?

Now, here are the 15 words for the word search puzzle based on the story:

E	E	T	A	L	A	P	L	M	I	X	L	C	S
P	L	A	C	A	T	P	A	S	S	I	O	N	U
E	O	U	R	T	I	F	O	R	P	N	O	N	O
R	N	T	A	S	T	A	N	D	A	R	D	S	A
F	M	O	F	M	C	E	T	R	I	N	A	C	M
E	E	M	T	E	C	N	E	L	L	E	C	X	E
C	T	O	S	F	E	I	C	A	R	S	E	C	C
T	I	T	M	O	E	N	I	S	I	U	C	T	S
I	C	I	A	C	O	M	M	I	T	M	E	N	T
O	U	V	N	A	A	R	P	R	N	S	N	T	R
N	L	E	S	E	D	U	C	A	T	I	O	N	C
T	O	N	H	F	U	N	D	R	A	I	S	E	R
M	U	O	I	A	L	I	T	P	O	E	R	A	R
N	S	I	P	P	R	E	C	I	S	I	O	N	L

PALATE
METICULOUS
EDUCATION
COMMITMENT
PRECISION
CARS
CRAFTSMANSHIP
AUTOMOTIVE
EXCELLENCE
STANDARDS
NONPROFIT
PASSION
FUNDRAISER
PERFECTION
CUISINE

"The story of Mr. Grant Money serves as a testament to the unwavering commitment to excellence, a commitment that knows no boundaries. From grant acquisition to automotive craftsmanship, from charity events to gourmet dining, Mr. Grant Money embodies the idea that pursuing perfection elevates every facet of life."

THE GRANT MAESTRO'S GRAND REVEAL

The Amazing Adventures of MRGRANTMONEY

The Grant Maestro's Grand Reveal: Secrets of $65 Million Success

A Keynote That Ignited Change - The Path to Urban Grant Acquisition Excellence

Mr. Grant Money, the epitome of elegance and style, took center stage as the keynote speaker at an upstate fundraiser. The event was a grand affair, attended by distinguished guests, philanthropists, and community leaders, all eager to hear Mr. Grant Money's wisdom and insights.

Dressed in a pinstriped dark navy blue suit, a regal cravat, a white ascot, and tan Italian shoes, Mr. Grant Money radiated an air of sophistication that captivated everyone in his presence. His cologne was a subtle yet intoxicating aura, enhancing his charm, style, and grace.

As Mr. Grant Money began to speak, the audience hung on his every word, eager to learn from the master of grant acquisition. He shared a remarkable story of helping a city secure $65 million in grant funding for a three-year transportation program, a feat that had transformed their infrastructure and improved the lives of their citizens.

With simplicity, clarity, and insight, Mr. Grant Money highlighted the key factors that had contributed to their success, leaving the audience spellbound:

1. Strategic Alignment: Mr. Grant Money emphasized the importance of aligning the city's transportation goals with the priorities of grant-making organizations. By demonstrating how their project aligned with regional and national objectives, they had made a compelling case for funding.

2. Data-Driven Approach: He spoke about the power of data and how meticulous research and analysis had played a crucial role. They had used data to identify areas with the greatest need for transportation improvements, presenting a well-supported case to potential funders.

3. Community Engagement: Mr. Grant Money stressed the significance of involving the community in the planning process. By actively engaging citizens and stakeholders, they had garnered support and demonstrated a commitment to addressing local concerns.

4. Collaborative Partnerships: He spoke of the importance of forging partnerships with other government agencies, nonprofits, and private sector entities. These collaborations had not only diversified funding sources but also strengthened their grant proposals.

5. Robust Grant Management: Mr. Grant Money underscored the need for effective grant management throughout the project's lifecycle. He explained how meticulous reporting, transparency, and accountability had built trust with funders and ensured the successful implementation of the program.

As Mr. Grant Money concluded his speech, the audience erupted in applause, inspired by his words of wisdom. However, among the attendees were a mayor and a city manager who had been whispering to each other throughout the keynote.

"Yes," the mayor said softly, "what he says is true, but what we really need is a Mr. Grant Money on our team."

The city manager nodded in agreement, and as Mr. Grant Money left the stage, they discreetly slipped a note into his hand, asking him to please call and help their cities.

With a knowing smile, Mr. Grant Money accepted the notes, fully aware that his expertise was in high demand. His mission to empower communities through grant acquisition had taken him to places far and wide, and there were many more adventures to come.

Exercise: "Mastering Urban Grant Acquisition Excellence"

This exercise will help you embrace key principles from Mr. Grant Money's grand reveal and apply them to your urban grant acquisition efforts. By focusing on strategic alignment, data-driven approaches, community engagement, collaborative partnerships, and robust grant management, you can improve your success in securing urban grants.

Objective: To develop a comprehensive approach to urban grant acquisition excellence that aligns with Mr. Grant Money's key principles.

Steps:

1. Defining Urban Grant Acquisition Goals:
- Identify the specific urban grant acquisition goals for your community or organization. What are the priority areas that require funding and improvement?

2. Strategic Alignment with Grant Priorities:
- Research grant-making organizations and funding opportunities to identify alignment with your urban goals. Create a clear connection between your project and the priorities of potential funders.

3. Data-Driven Analysis:
- Invest in data collection and analysis to understand the unique needs of your urban area. Use data to make a compelling case for grant funding and demonstrate the impact of your project.

4. Community Engagement Strategy:
- Develop a comprehensive plan for involving the urban community in the grant acquisition process. Hold town hall meetings, solicit feedback, and demonstrate a commitment to addressing local concerns.

5. Collaborative Partnerships:
- Identify potential partners from other government agencies, nonprofits, and the private sector. Explore opportunities for collaboration to strengthen grant proposals and diversify funding sources.

6. Effective Grant Management:
- Establish a robust grant management system that includes detailed reporting, transparency, and accountability. Showcase your commitment to responsible fund usage to build trust with funders.

7. Case Study Review:
- Study successful urban grant acquisition case studies to gain insights into how other communities have achieved grant funding. Analyze their strategies and adapt them to your specific context.

8. Preparation of Grant Proposals:
- Begin crafting grant proposals with a strong focus on the principles of alignment, data, community engagement, partnerships, and effective management. Ensure each proposal reflects the specific needs of your urban project.

9. Review and Feedback:
- Seek feedback from peers, mentors, or colleagues with experience in urban grant acquisition. Use their input to refine your grant proposals and strategies.

10. Continual Improvement:
- Commit to continuous improvement in your grant acquisition efforts. Regularly update your goals, strategies, and approaches based on evolving urban needs and available grant opportunities.

11. Networking and Collaboration:
- Attend urban-focused grant acquisition events, seminars, and conferences to network with experts and potential partners. Foster collaborations to strengthen your grant acquisition efforts.

By following this exercise, you will enhance your urban grant acquisition strategies by incorporating Mr. Grant Money's principles. The path to urban grant acquisition excellence involves careful alignment, data-driven insights, community engagement, collaboration, and effective management, and your efforts will lead to the transformation and improvement of your urban community.

Discussion Questions

1. Mr. Grant Money's keynote emphasized the importance of strategic alignment in grant acquisition. How can organizations effectively align their project goals with the priorities of grant-making organizations, and what benefits can this alignment bring to the grant-seeking process?

2. Data-driven approaches played a crucial role in securing $65 million in grant funding. How can organizations utilize data to support their grant proposals and demonstrate the need for their projects? What are some best practices for effective data analysis in grant acquisition?

3. Community engagement and collaboration were highlighted as significant factors in grant acquisition success. How can organizations actively involve their communities and build collaborative partnerships to strengthen their grant applications and win the support of funders? What challenges might organizations encounter in these efforts?

4. The speech stressed the importance of robust grant management throughout the project's lifecycle. How can organizations establish effective grant management practices to ensure the successful implementation of funded projects, maintain transparency, and build trust with funders? What strategies can they employ to overcome common grant management challenges?

5. Mr. Grant Money's expertise and reputation as a grant acquisition specialist are evident in the mayor and city manager's desire to have him on their team. What key qualities or skills make a grant acquisition expert valuable to organizations seeking grants? How can organizations identify and work with experienced grant specialists to improve their grant success rates?

💡 **Big Idea** "The Annual Grant Wisdom Symposium"

Create a yearly event called the "Annual Grant Wisdom Symposium" inspired by Mr. Grant Money's philosophy of learning from every adventure. This symposium would bring together seasoned grant acquisition specialists, philanthropists, and organizations to share their insights and experiences. Participants would not only learn about successful grant strategies but also have the opportunity to reflect on the broader lessons that can be applied to life and work. It would be an unconventional, cross-disciplinary platform for exchanging wisdom and strategies for grant acquisition and personal development..

🔍 Word Search

Step into the world of Mr. Grant Money, a symbol of elegance, wisdom, and grant acquisition expertise. Join us on a journey of words as we explore the essential elements that make Mr. Grant Money the master of his craft.

In this puzzle, discover the words related to the extraordinary adventures of Mr. Grant Money. Can you find all the hidden words that capture the essence of this remarkable story?

Now, here are the 14 words for the word search puzzle based on the story:

Y	G	P	E	I	N	P	E	T	P	P	E	F	T
U	C	A	U	E	I	H	X	P	R	A	R	U	N
A	D	R	E	N	E	I	P	N	H	T	A	N	E
T	M	T	Y	R	N	L	E	E	V	I	A	D	M
N	C	N	S	D	G	A	R	V	G	E	A	R	E
E	M	E	U	E	A	N	T	I	A	M	Y	A	G
M	E	R	C	U	G	T	I	R	E	O	T	I	A
N	M	S	C	D	E	H	S	D	L	D	I	S	N
G	P	H	E	S	M	R	E	A	E	S	N	E	A
I	O	I	S	T	E	O	P	T	G	I	U	R	M
L	W	P	S	Y	N	P	L	A	A	W	M	N	H
A	E	S	N	L	T	I	A	D	N	E	M	E	M
N	R	O	A	E	W	S	H	I	C	E	O	P	N
I	H	E	H	E	E	T	O	N	E	S	C	N	V

EXPERTISE
FUNDRAISER
COMMUNITY
ENGAGEMENT
PHILANTHROPIST
STYLE
ALIGNMENT
MANAGEMENT
PARTNERSHIPS
EMPOWER
WISDOM
DATA-DRIVEN
ELEGANCE
SUCCESS

"Mr. Grant Money isn't just a speaker; he's a catalyst for change. His wisdom doesn't just inspire; it ignites action, making the impossible possible."
-Mr. Grant Money

TAKING THE LEAP

Taking the Leap: Mr. Grant Money's Airborne Epiphany

From Parachutes to Philanthropy - Insights for Success

High above the picturesque landscape of Molalla, Oregon, Mr. Grant Money soared thousands of feet in the air, ready for his 37th parachute jump. He had undertaken many adventures in his life, but there was something uniquely exhilarating about leaping from a classic aircraft into the open sky.

The panoramic view below showcased the stunning beauty of Oregon's wilderness, a patchwork of lush green forests and rolling hills. As the wind rushed past him, Mr. Grant Money felt a sense of courage and confidence in his plan. He had meticulously prepared for this jump, just as he did for every venture in his life.

As he descended, his mind was a whirlwind of calculations and procedures. The steps for a safe landing had become second nature, ingrained in his mind like a well-practiced habit. He knew that to ensure a smooth and graceful landing, every detail mattered.

His chute billowed above him, gently guiding him toward the earth. Mr. Grant Money couldn't help but think about all the things he must do right in these final moments. It was a process he had systemized in his mind, and he trusted in his training and experience.

But there was one thing he had learned from his 37th jump, something that he hinted at but didn't reveal until later. It was a flash of insight, a valuable lesson that had become a part of his personal philosophy.

As the ground approached, Mr. Grant Money made his final adjustments, ensuring a perfect landing. With elegance and style that were second nature to him, he touched down on the soft, welcoming earth.

Always prepared, he reached into his gear and pulled out his treasured notebook. With a flourish of his pen, he recorded his message and added another bit of insight that he would share with his next client. He wrote:

"In every jump, as in life, success is in the details. From the first step to the final landing, it's the meticulous preparation, the unwavering focus, and the commitment to excellence that lead to a safe and graceful descent. Remember, my friends, every adventure is an opportunity to learn, and every landing is a chance to rise again."

With those words, Mr. Grant Money closed his notebook and tucked it away, ready for the next adventure and the next opportunity to share his wisdom. His amazing adventures were a testament to his courage, confidence, and the valuable insights he gathered along the way, all in the pursuit of helping charities and government agencies secure the funding they needed to make a difference in the world.

Exercise: "The Leap to Grant Acquisition Excellence"

This exercise draws inspiration from Mr. Grant Money's airborne epiphany and focuses on adopting a methodical approach to grant acquisition, much like his preparation for parachute jumps. By embracing meticulous preparation, unwavering focus, and a commitment to excellence, you can enhance your grant acquisition skills.

Objective: To develop a structured process for grant acquisition excellence by focusing on preparation, attention to detail, and continuous learning.

Steps:

1. Define Your Grant Acquisition Goals:
- Clearly define the grant acquisition goals for your organization or cause. What specific funding do you need, and how will it make a difference in your mission?

2. Meticulous Preparation:
- Develop a step-by-step plan for your grant acquisition journey. Identify the essential tasks, deadlines, and resources required to execute the plan successfully.

3. Grant Research and Analysis:
- Systematically research available grants and funding opportunities. Analyze their eligibility criteria, priorities, and alignment with your goals.

4. Focused Proposal Development:
- Craft tailored grant proposals that directly address the interests and priorities of potential funders. Pay meticulous attention to the details and quality of your proposals.

5. Data-Driven Insights:
- Utilize data to support your grant applications. Showcase the impact and outcomes of your project using quantifiable evidence to strengthen your case.

6. Project Readiness:
- Ensure that your organization is fully prepared to execute the proposed project. Have a detailed implementation plan, team, and resources in place.

7. Continuous Learning and Adaptation:

- Treat every grant application as an opportunity to learn. Analyze feedback and rejections to make improvements for future proposals.

8.Focus on Excellence:

- Maintain an unwavering commitment to excellence in all grant acquisition activities. Pay attention to every detail and strive for the highest quality.

9. Tracking and Reporting:

- Implement a system for tracking grant applications, responses, and outcomes. Prepare clear and concise reports for funders during and after the project.

10. Networking and Professional Development:

- Engage with other grant acquisition professionals, attend workshops, and seek opportunities to improve your grant acquisition skills.

11. Reflect and Adapt:

- After each grant application cycle, reflect on your experiences, lessons learned, and outcomes. Use this reflection to adapt and refine your approach.

12. Share Your Insights:

- Just as Mr. Grant Money shared his insight with his clients, consider sharing your lessons and experiences with peers or within your organization. Mentor others in their grant acquisition journey.

By following these steps, you can develop a structured and systematic approach to grant acquisition that emphasizes meticulous preparation, unwavering focus, and a commitment to excellence. This approach will help you maximize your chances of securing grants and making a positive impact on your organization or cause.

Discussion Questions

1. Mr. Grant Money's parachute jump experience emphasized the importance of meticulous preparation in every endeavor. How can organizations apply this lesson to their grant acquisition efforts? What are the key elements of preparation and planning that contribute to success in grant applications?

2. Mr. Grant Money's insight mentioned that "success is in the details." What strategies can organizations use to pay attention to the finer details in their grant proposals and applications? How can they ensure that their submissions are not only well-prepared but also stand out to grant-making organizations?

3. In his message, Mr. Grant Money stressed the value of learning from every adventure. How can organizations adopt a culture of continuous learning and improvement in their grant-seeking processes? What mechanisms can they put in place to gather insights from past applications and experiences?

4. The idea of a "graceful descent" was highlighted in Mr. Grant Money's message. How can organizations ensure a graceful and successful outcome, not only in securing grants but also in implementing and managing the funded projects? What best practices should they follow for a smooth landing in their grant-funded endeavors?

5. Mr. Grant Money's notebook message encouraged individuals to "rise again" after every landing. How can organizations build resilience and adaptability into their grant-seeking strategies, allowing them to persist and improve even in the face of challenges and setbacks? What role does resilience play in long-term grant acquisition success.

💡 **Big Idea** "The Global Grant Writing Challenge"

Organize an annual worldwide competition, named the "Global Grant Writing Challenge," inspired by Mr. Grant Money's mission to empower others. Open to individuals and organizations, this challenge would invite participants to create grant proposals for real-world projects. The top submissions would receive funding for their projects, creating a practical approach to learning grant writing while making a positive impact. The competition encourages innovation, creativity, and collaboration, turning grant writing into an exciting endeavor and fostering global change.

🔍 Word Search

Join Mr. Grant Money on an aerial adventure like no other as he soars through the skies of Molalla, Oregon. In this word search puzzle, you'll discover the words and principles that make Mr. Grant Money's parachute jump a metaphor for his grant acquisition success.

In this puzzle, discover the words related to the extraordinary adventures of Mr. Grant Money. Can you find all the hidden words that capture the essence of this remarkable story?

Now, here are the 14 words for the word search puzzle based on the story:

L	A	N	D	I	N	G	C	D	M	O	C	D	C
A	A	S	E	U	M	T	H	G	I	S	N	I	C
U	L	I	P	T	E	T	U	H	C	A	R	A	P
T	N	E	M	T	I	M	M	O	C	P	D	C	E
N	A	E	E	E	S	I	C	E	G	A	P	S	C
S	D	S	P	C	U	T	L	H	S	A	R	Y	N
I	V	U	E	T	O	F	D	T	U	S	E	S	A
M	E	X	C	E	L	L	E	N	C	E	P	T	G
W	N	A	D	C	U	E	T	G	O	I	A	E	E
I	T	U	L	P	C	R	A	U	F	U	R	M	L
S	U	O	E	C	I	O	I	U	U	C	E	I	E
D	R	F	E	S	T	Y	L	E	P	C	D	Z	Y
O	E	T	D	I	E	I	S	E	C	A	G	E	I
M	L	E	E	R	M	E	T	A	L	X	Y	D	T

METICULOUS
EXCELLENCE
INSIGHT
PARACHUTE
WISDOM
STYLE
ELEGANCE
PREPARED
SYSTEMIZED
COMMITMENT
DETAILS
FOCUS
LANDING
ADVENTURE

"Mr. Grant Money's parachute jump is a metaphor for life and success. Every venture we undertake, whether it's a literal leap from an airplane or the pursuit of grant funding, demands precision, commitment, and the courage to rise, even after we've landed. Success is in the details."

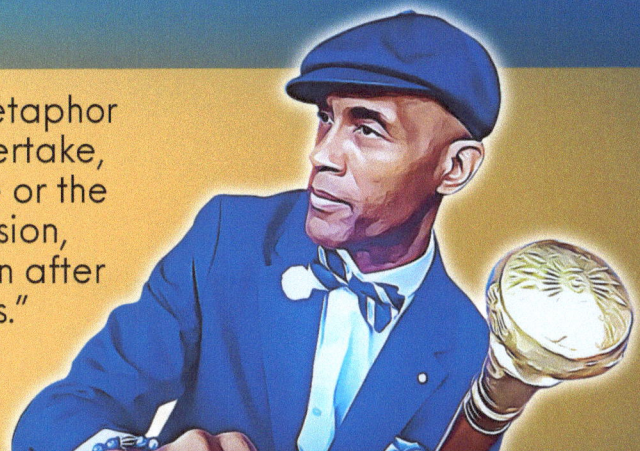

RHYTHMS OF IMPACT

The Amazing Adventures of **MRGRANTMONEY**

Rhythms of Impact: Mr. Grant Money's Journey to Empowerment

Grant Writing Mastery Unleashed - A Tale of Cuban Inspiration and Innovation

In a remote and picturesque part of Cuba, Mr. Grant Money embarked on a mission that would multiply his impact and help countless nonprofits, government agencies, faith-based organizations, and educational institutions secure the funding they needed. It was a journey of innovation, education, and a touch of Cuban flair.

Surrounded by the vibrant culture of Havana and its classic old-school cars, Mr. Grant Money and his team meticulously developed a program that would soon become renowned as "Grant Writing That Gets Funded" nationwide training through Grant Central USA. While Mr. Grant Money himself didn't indulge in smoking, the analogy was apt: the course was crafted with the precision and artistry of a finely made Cuban cigar.

This special training was designed to provide numerous life-changing benefits for each student who enrolled. Mr. Grant Money understood that by multiplying his knowledge and expertise, he could empower individuals from all walks of life to master the art of grant writing and acquisition. It was his way of sharing the secret to success and making a lasting impact on the world of grants.

As word spread about the course, students from across the nation flocked to major universities where top-notch experienced instructors led the classes. The program covered everything from the fundamentals of grant writing to the intricacies of relationship building with funders. It was a comprehensive curriculum that left no stone unturned.

During his time in Cuba, Mr. Grant Money couldn't help but notice the admiration he received from the local ladies. They whispered to each other about his impeccable style, which seemed to fit elegantly with the classic cars that graced the streets of Havana. One of them even hinted at wanting to dance with him, their moves matching the rhythm of the Cuban music that filled the air.

But Mr. Grant Money, cool and self-assured as always, chose to focus on the matter at hand. He had a mission to accomplish, one that would generate millions of dollars for countless organizations. Dancing would have to wait for another time.

As the course continued to thrive and multiply across the country, Mr. Grant Money knew he had made the right decision. His legacy would be not only the grants he secured but also the knowledge and expertise he shared with others. Through "Grant Writing That Gets Funded," he was creating a ripple effect of change that would touch the lives of many and make the world a better place, one grant at a time.

And so, with a sense of purpose and a touch of Cuban inspiration, Mr. Grant Money continued his amazing adventures, leaving a trail of empowered grant writers and transformed organizations in his wake.

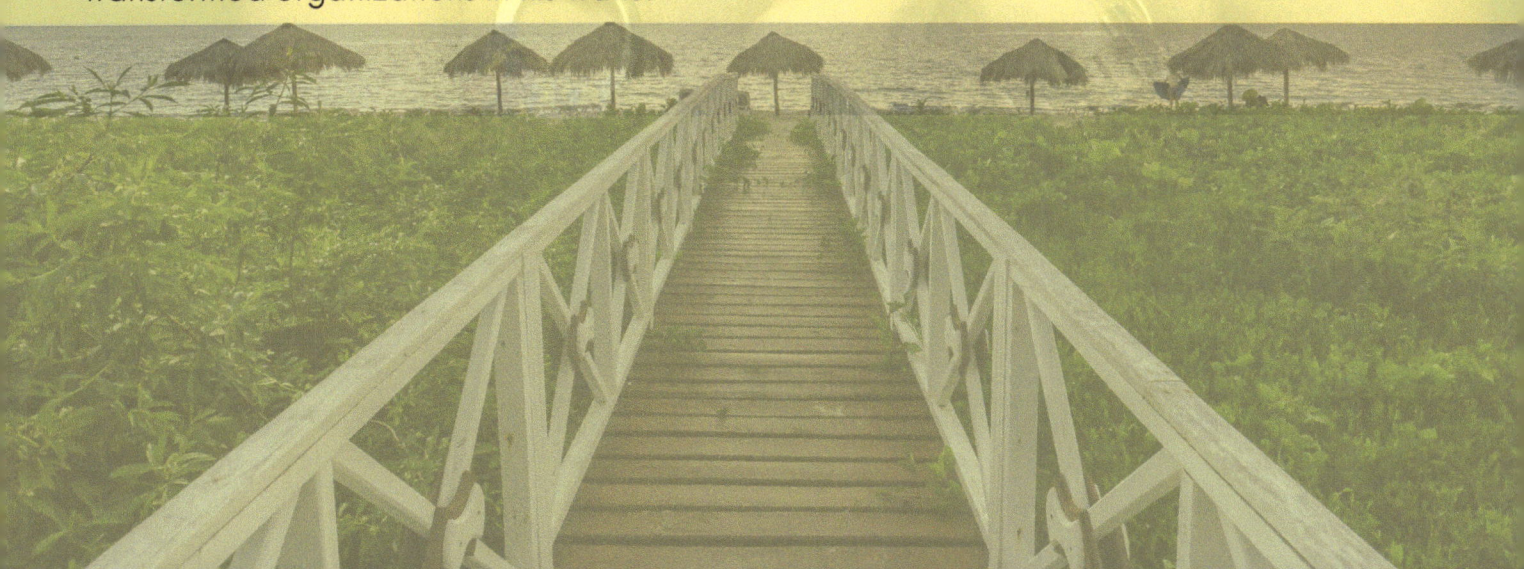

Exercise: "Empower Through Education: Create Your Own Mini Grant Writing Workshop"

Inspired by Mr. Grant Money's mission to empower others through grant writing training, this exercise allows you to share your grant writing expertise and make a positive impact on those around you.

Objective: Develop and host a mini grant writing workshop to empower individuals to master the art of grant writing, just as Mr. Grant Money did with "Grant Writing That Gets Funded."

Steps:

1. Define Your Workshop Objectives:
- Determine the specific objectives of your mini grant writing workshop. What do you want participants to learn and achieve by the end of the workshop?

2. Identify Your Target Audience:
- Decide who your workshop is intended for. It could be aspiring grant writers, volunteers, employees of nonprofit organizations, or anyone interested in learning about grant writing.

3. Select a Workshop Format:
- Choose the format of your workshop. Will it be a one-day event, a series of sessions, or an online workshop? Consider what best suits your audience.

4. Prepare Workshop Materials:
- Develop comprehensive workshop materials, including presentations, handouts, sample grant proposals, and exercises. Ensure that the content covers grant writing fundamentals.

5. Arrange a Suitable Venue:
- Secure a venue for your workshop. Depending on your audience size and budget, this could be a local community center, library, or even an online platform.

6. Promote Your Workshop:
- Create promotional materials such as flyers, social media posts, and email invitations. Encourage participants to register in advance.

7. Craft an Engaging Agenda:
- Outline a detailed agenda for your workshop. Include topics like understanding grant opportunities, proposal writing, budgeting, and relationship building with funders.

8. Conduct the Workshop:
- Deliver your mini grant writing workshop, engaging participants through interactive sessions, discussions, and practical exercises. Encourage questions and foster a collaborative learning environment.

9. Share Your Knowledge:
- Share your insights and practical tips on grant writing, just as Mr. Grant Money shared his expertise. Provide guidance on how to approach grant proposals and build relationships with potential funders.

10. Review Sample Grant Proposals:
- Share and discuss sample grant proposals with your participants. Analyze what makes these proposals effective and encourage participants to practice writing their own.

11. Offer Feedback and Guidance:
- Provide constructive feedback to participants on their grant proposals and encourage revisions for improvement. Share best practices and common pitfalls to avoid.

12. Networking and Collaboration:
- Encourage networking among participants. Building connections with others interested in grant writing can lead to future collaboration and support.

13. Collect Feedback:
- At the end of your workshop, ask for feedback from participants. Use this feedback to improve future workshops and ensure that the needs of your audience are met.

14. Encourage Participants to Empower Others:
- Inspire your workshop attendees to share their newly acquired grant writing knowledge with others, creating a ripple effect of empowerment in your community.

By conducting your mini grant writing workshop, you can empower individuals to make a positive impact on their communities and causes they care about, just as Mr. Grant Money did through "Grant Writing That Gets Funded." Your efforts will create a ripple effect of change in the world of grants, one workshop at a time.

Discussion Questions

1. Mr. Grant Money's training program, "Grant Writing That Gets Funded," had a significant impact on individuals and organizations. How can this story inspire a discussion about the importance of education and training in the field of grant acquisition? What are the key components of an effective grant writing program, and how can such initiatives empower individuals and communities?

2. The story highlights Mr. Grant Money's focus and dedication to his mission despite the distractions around him. How can this narrative prompt a conversation about the importance of staying committed to a goal and managing distractions in grant acquisition efforts? What strategies can individuals and organizations employ to maintain their focus and drive in the competitive world of grants?

3. The story mentions the "ripple effect of change" that Mr. Grant Money's training program created. How can organizations measure the impact of their grant acquisition efforts beyond the immediate grant funding? What are some examples of the broader impact that successful grants can have on communities, and how can this be quantified or communicated?

4. The Cuban culture and music play a role in the story. How can cultural influences and local context affect grant acquisition strategies? What considerations should organizations keep in mind when working in diverse cultural settings and how can they leverage cultural elements to strengthen their grant proposals?

5. Mr. Grant Money's approach involves sharing his expertise and empowering others. How can mentorship and knowledge sharing be incorporated into grant acquisition strategies? What benefits can individuals and organizations gain from mentoring relationships, and how can they go about establishing and maintaining such connections?

💡 Big Idea "Aerial Grant Webinars with a View"

Offer grant webinars conducted from hot air balloons or unique locations with breathtaking views. As an innovative twist on traditional webinars, these sessions would provide practical insights into grants, grant writing and acquisition while surrounded by natural beauty or captivating landscapes. Whether it's a balloon in the sky or a picturesque mountain setting, participants can join virtually from around the world, combining learning with inspiration.

🔍 Word Search

Step into the world of Mr. Grant Money and his mission to revolutionize grant writing. Amid the vibrant culture of Cuba, he developed a program that would empower countless individuals to master the art of grant acquisition.

In this puzzle, discover the words related to the extraordinary adventures of Mr. Grant Money. Can you find all the hidden words that capture the essence of this remarkable story?

Now, here are the 15 words for the word search puzzle based on the story:

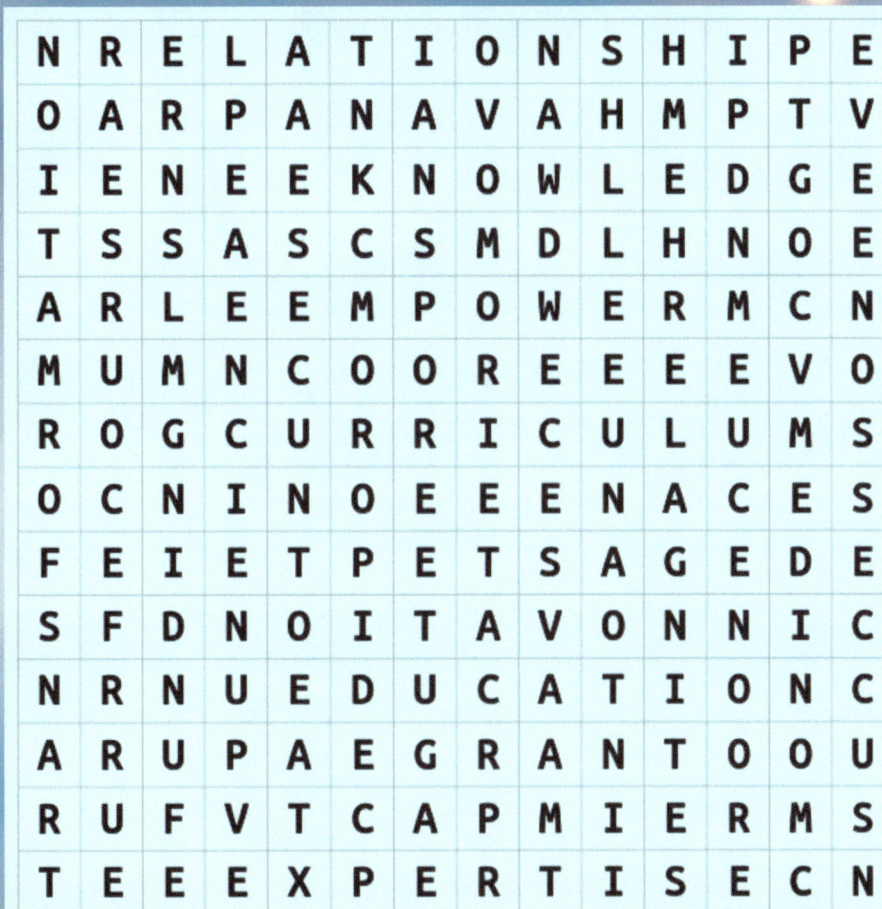

N	R	E	L	A	T	I	O	N	S	H	I	P	E
O	A	R	P	A	N	A	V	A	H	M	P	T	V
I	E	N	E	E	K	N	O	W	L	E	D	G	E
T	S	S	A	S	C	S	M	D	L	H	N	O	E
A	R	L	E	E	M	P	O	W	E	R	M	C	N
M	U	M	N	C	O	O	R	E	E	E	E	V	O
R	O	G	C	U	R	R	I	C	U	L	U	M	S
O	C	N	I	N	O	E	E	E	N	A	C	E	S
F	E	I	E	T	P	E	T	S	A	G	E	D	E
S	F	D	N	O	I	T	A	V	O	N	N	I	C
N	R	N	U	E	D	U	C	A	T	I	O	N	C
A	R	U	P	A	E	G	R	A	N	T	O	O	U
R	U	F	V	T	C	A	P	M	I	E	R	M	S
T	E	E	E	X	P	E	R	T	I	S	E	C	N

FUNDING
KNOWLEDGE
GRANT
RELATIONSHIP
EDUCATION
CURRICULUM
EXPERTISE
HAVANA
SECRET
TRANSFORMATION
SUCCESS
COURSE
INNOVATION
EMPOWER
IMPACT

"Just as the rhythm of Cuban music fills the air in Havana, the rhythm of grant writing is about understanding the steps, mastering the moves, and hitting the right notes. With the right education and dedication, you can dance your way to grant acquisition success."

-Mr. Grant Money

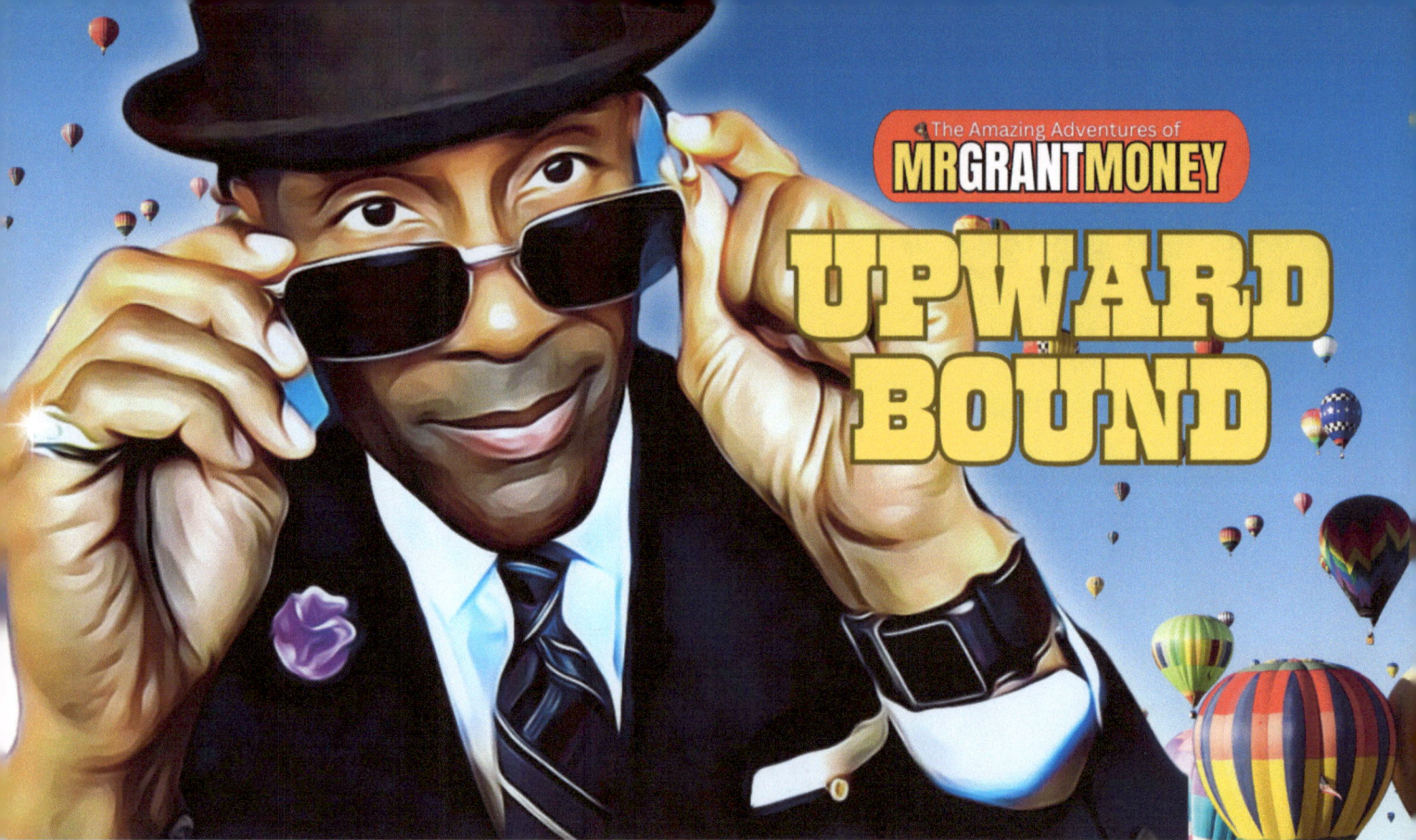

UPWARD BOUND

Grant Money's Upward Bound: Soaring with Balloons in Albuquerque

*Inspiration from Above - How Balloon Flights
Echo Grant Success*

In the vibrant city of Albuquerque, New Mexico, in the heart of October, Mr. Grant Money found himself at the University of New Mexico for a Grant Mastery Training. The air was tinged with excitement and a sense of wonder, for it was also the time of the Albuquerque International Balloon Fiesta—a spectacle that drew visitors from around the world to witness the breathtaking sight of colorful balloons ascending into the clear New Mexico skies.

As Mr. Grant Money explored the city during his free time, he couldn't help but be drawn to the festivities of the balloon fiesta. The energy in the air was infectious, and he found himself chatting with locals and tourists alike, all united by their love for the majestic balloons that filled the sky.

One day, while strolling through the fiesta grounds, he struck up a conversation with a photographer named Charlie, who had traveled all the way from Australia to capture the beauty of the event through his lens. Charlie explained that he was particularly interested in photographing a balloon sponsored by a corporate entity, a sight he found intriguing.

As fate would have it, Charlie had met the pilot of one such balloon, Aaron, who was more than willing to accommodate the extra space on their flight. They saw an opportunity in inviting Mr. Grant Money to join them, hoping to gain insight and perhaps secure additional funding for their balloon endeavors.

With his characteristic charm and curiosity, Mr. Grant Money accepted their invitation without hesitation. The idea of ascending into the New Mexico sky in a colorful balloon appealed to his adventurous spirit, and he knew that every experience held the potential for fresh perspectives.

As the balloon gently rose into the crisp morning air, Mr. Grant Money couldn't help but be captivated by the breathtaking view. The vast expanse of the New Mexico landscape stretched out below, a patchwork of colors and textures that mirrored the diversity of grant acquisition.

As he observed the teamwork between the pilot, Aaron, and the corporate sponsors, he couldn't help but draw parallels to the world of grants. The collaboration, communication, and careful planning that went into making the balloon flight a success mirrored the elements that were crucial in securing grant funding.

High above Albuquerque, Mr. Grant Money found a sense of serenity and inspiration. He reached into his pocket and retrieved his treasured notebook, which he often referred to as his "Gold-Mine" of insights. With the awe-inspiring scenery as his backdrop, he penned his thoughts:

"From the heights of innovation to the depths of collaboration, every endeavor holds the potential for success. Just as a balloon soars with the support of sponsors, grants too rely on strong partnerships and shared visions. Remember, my friends, that in every journey, there are lessons to be learned, and every experience is a chance to gain fresh perspectives."

As the balloon descended back to Earth, Mr. Grant Money shared his insights with Charlie and Aaron. They appreciated his wisdom greatly, and in the spirit of camaraderie, Charlie extended an invitation for Mr. Grant Money to visit Australia, where he could share his expertise with a new audience.

With a smile and a nod, Mr. Grant Money accepted the invitation, for he knew that his journey to help charities and government agencies secure funding was a global endeavor, and every adventure held the potential for transformation and inspiration, no matter where it took him.

Exercise: "Gaining Fresh Perspectives: A Grant Acquisition Adventure"

This exercise is inspired by Mr. Grant Money's experience during the Albuquerque International Balloon Fiesta and encourages you to seek fresh perspectives and lessons for grant acquisition through a unique adventure.

Objective: To gain new insights and perspectives for grant acquisition by engaging in an unfamiliar and exciting activity.

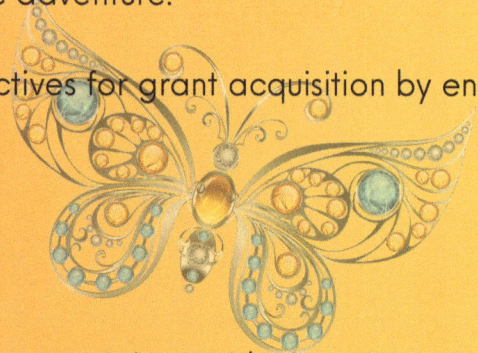

Steps:

1. Choose an Unfamiliar Adventure:
- Select an activity or adventure you've never experienced before. It could be a hot air balloon ride, hiking a challenging trail, visiting an art gallery, or anything that you find exciting.

2. Research and Prepare:
- Research the chosen adventure to understand its basics and safety guidelines. Make the necessary preparations to ensure a safe and enjoyable experience.

3. Experience the Adventure:
- Participate in the adventure with an open mind and a willingness to absorb new perspectives. Embrace the experience fully and be present in the moment.

4. Observe and Reflect:
- While engaging in the adventure, pay attention to the details and experiences. Observe how teamwork, planning, and communication play a role in the activity.

5. Connect the Dots:
- After completing the adventure, take time to connect the lessons learned from the experience to the world of grant acquisition. Consider how elements like collaboration, innovation, and shared visions in the adventure can be applied to grant-seeking endeavors.

6. Capture Your Insights:

- Record your thoughts and insights in a dedicated journal or notebook. Much like Mr. Grant Money's treasured notebook, use this journal to document your newfound perspectives.

7. Share Your Insights:

- Share your adventure and the insights gained with friends, colleagues, or fellow grant seekers. Engage in discussions to foster new ideas and perspectives.

8. Apply the Lessons:

- Identify how the lessons from your adventure can be applied to your grant acquisition efforts. Whether it's strengthening partnerships, approaching challenges innovatively, or enhancing communication, put your insights into action.

9. Expand Your Horizons:

- Consider taking this exercise to a global level by exploring opportunities to share your insights and expertise with a new audience, as Mr. Grant Money did by accepting the invitation to visit Australia.

10. Reflect on Your Impact:

- Keep a record of any positive changes or improvements in your grant acquisition activities resulting from the fresh perspectives gained during your adventure.

This exercise encourages you to break out of your routine and seek inspiration and lessons from unique experiences, just as Mr. Grant Money did during the balloon fiesta. The lessons and insights you gather can lead to innovative approaches and a renewed sense of purpose in your grant acquisition efforts.

> "Like a colorful balloon ascending into the New Mexico skies, the journey of grant acquisition is a beautiful and adventurous one. It's about collaboration, innovation, and reaching new heights, supported by sponsors who believe in your vision."
> -Mr. Grant Money

Discussion Questions

1. The story draws parallels between the teamwork and planning involved in hot air balloon flights and the grant acquisition process. How can this analogy serve as a starting point for discussing the importance of collaboration and preparation in grant acquisition? What lessons can individuals and organizations in the grant world learn from the world of balloon flights?

2. Mr. Grant Money mentions gaining "fresh perspectives" from every experience. How can this narrative prompt a discussion on the value of seeking new perspectives in grant acquisition? What strategies or approaches can grant seekers use to broaden their horizons, whether through new experiences or diverse perspectives, and how can this positively impact their grant acquisition efforts?

3. The story highlights Mr. Grant Money's willingness to accept an invitation to visit Australia and share his expertise. How can this lead to a conversation about the global nature of grant acquisition and the potential for international collaboration? What are the opportunities and challenges in expanding grant acquisition efforts beyond one's own community or country?

4. Mr. Grant Money refers to his notebook as his "Gold-Mine" of insights. How can this encourage a discussion about the importance of keeping records, documenting experiences, and maintaining a learning mindset in the field of grants? What are some best practices for effective note-taking and knowledge-sharing in grant acquisition?

5. The Albuquerque International Balloon Fiesta is described as an event that brings people together from around the world. How can this story be a starting point for discussing the role of community and connections in grant acquisition? What are the benefits of building a network of grant acquisition professionals and fostering relationships with potential funders, and how can individuals and organizations effectively engage with their communities to enhance their grant efforts?

💡 Big Idea "Mr. Grant Money's Legacy Notebook Exchange"

Establish a unique network or platform where grant professionals can exchange their own "gold notebooks" or notebooks filled with valuable insights and lessons learned from their grant acquisition journeys. This exchange would allow grant writers to benefit from the experiences of their peers, gaining access to practical tips, successful strategies, and motivational notes. This collaborative approach to knowledge sharing could become a valuable resource for grant seekers worldwide.

🔍 Word Search

Step into the world of Mr. Grant Money's adventures and discover the words associated with his journey in the vibrant city of Albuquerque, New Mexico. Amidst the excitement of the Albuquerque International Balloon Fiesta, Mr. Grant Money finds inspiration and new perspectives as he takes to the skies.

In this puzzle, discover the words related to the extraordinary adventures of Mr. Grant Money. Can you find all the hidden words that capture the essence of this remarkable story?

Now, here are the 14 words for the word search puzzle based on the story:

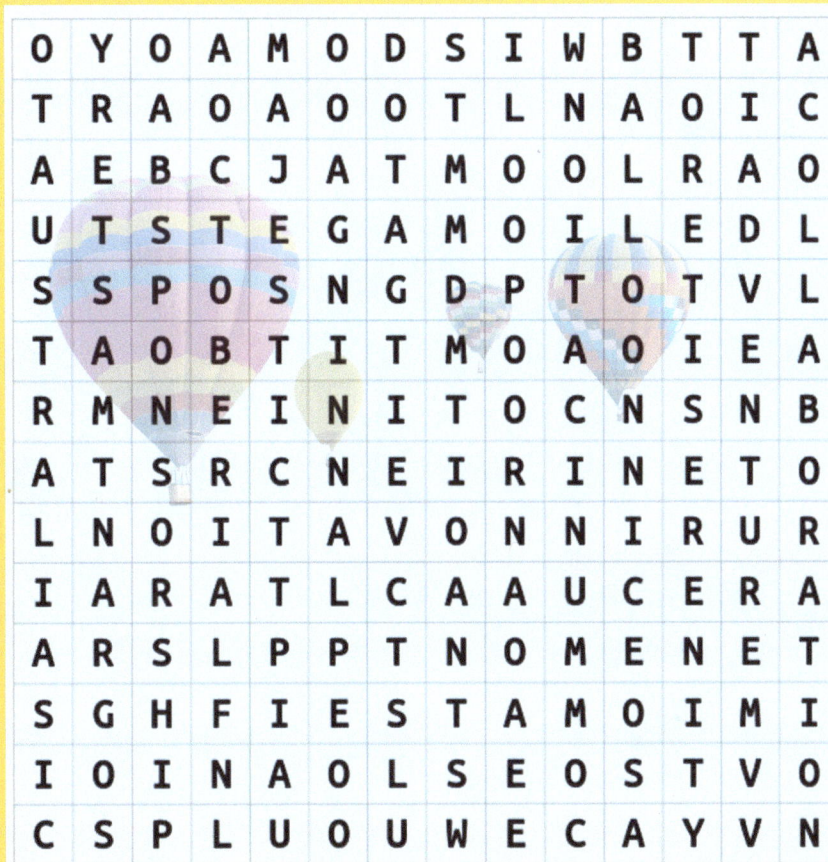

O	Y	O	A	M	O	D	S	I	W	B	T	T	A
T	R	A	O	A	O	O	T	L	N	A	O	I	C
A	E	B	C	J	A	T	M	O	O	L	R	A	O
U	T	S	T	E	G	A	M	O	I	L	E	D	L
S	S	P	O	S	N	G	D	P	T	O	T	V	L
T	A	O	B	T	I	T	M	O	A	O	I	E	A
R	M	N	E	I	N	I	T	O	C	N	S	N	B
A	T	S	R	C	N	E	I	R	I	N	E	T	O
L	N	O	I	T	A	V	O	N	N	I	R	U	R
I	A	R	A	T	L	C	A	A	U	C	E	R	A
A	R	S	L	P	P	T	N	O	M	E	N	E	T
S	G	H	F	I	E	S	T	A	M	O	I	M	I
I	O	I	N	A	O	L	S	E	O	S	T	V	O
C	S	P	L	U	O	U	W	E	C	A	Y	V	N

BALLOON
WISDOM
SERENITY
INNOVATION
SPONSORSHIP
AUSTRALIA
PLANNING
FIESTA
OCTOBER
COLLABORATION
GRANT MASTERY
ADVENTURE
MAJESTIC
COMMUNICATION

"Mr. Grant Money's journey above Albuquerque serves as a reminder that inspiration can be found in unexpected places. It's a testament to the power of collaboration and shared experiences, demonstrating that every adventure, whether on the ground or in the sky, has the potential to create lasting connections and inspiration."

ALAMO EPIPHANY

The Alamo Epiphany: Mr. Grant Money's Insights on Grant Acquisition

Unearthing Grant Wisdom Amidst Texas History

In the historic city of San Antonio, Mr. Grant Money found himself at the renowned Alamo, a symbol of Texas history and bravery. However, to his surprise, he wasn't as impressed with the site as some might expect. His sentiments about the Alamo were about as indifferent as Charles Barkley's infamous comment about the women of San Antonio, though Mr. Grant Money had no such reservations about the city's inhabitants.

After his visit to the Alamo, Mr. Grant Money decided to explore the charm of San Antonio's Riverwalk, a picturesque waterway lined with restaurants, shops, and lush greenery. He settled into a quaint Mexican restaurant, savoring the rich flavors of the cuisine as small boats sailed by, carrying tourists and locals alike.

While enjoying his meal, Mr. Grant Money took a moment to delve into a book he had brought along, "The Magic of Thinking Big" by David J. Schwartz. The book's timeless wisdom resonated with him, and he couldn't help but think about how several nonprofits and city governments could benefit from its important lessons.

As he read, Mr. Grant Money noted five direct lessons from the book that he believed were essential for those seeking grant funding. With a sense of purpose, he penned them into his trusted gold notebook:

1. Believe in Your Vision: Mr. Grant Money recognized that to secure grants, organizations must first believe in the importance of their mission and vision. Confidence in their cause would be the driving force behind their grant-seeking efforts.

2. Set Ambitious Goals: He emphasized the need for nonprofits and city governments to set ambitious, yet achievable goals. Funders were more likely to support projects that aimed high and promised significant impact.

3. Cultivate a Positive Attitude: Mr. Grant Money underlined the importance of maintaining a positive attitude throughout the grant-seeking process. A can-do spirit would not only attract funders but also inspire confidence in potential partners and collaborators.

4. Take Decisive Action: He noted that action was the key to success. Organizations needed to take decisive steps, be proactive in their grant acquisition efforts, and seek out opportunities with determination.

5. Learn from Setbacks: Mr. Grant Money recognized that setbacks were a natural part of the grant-seeking journey. Rather than being discouraged by rejection, organizations should view it as an opportunity to learn and refine their approach.

As Mr. Grant Money closed the book, his thoughts turned to one of his earliest successes—a $400,000 grant that he had helped one of his first clients secure. He knew that the lessons he had just noted were instrumental in that achievement.

With a chuckle, he thought out loud, "If I ever lost this gold notebook, someone would have all they need to win BIG in securing grants." But then, with a wry smile, he added, "But I'm not planning on ever losing it. This is my gold-mine!"

With his gold notebook safely tucked away, Mr. Grant Money continued to travel the world, armed with knowledge, experience, and a passion for helping charities and government agencies secure the funding they needed to make a difference in their communities.

Exercise: "The Alamo Epiphany - Grant Success through Thinking Big"

This exercise is designed to help individuals and organizations in their grant-seeking endeavors by adopting the key lessons shared by Mr. Grant Money from "The Magic of Thinking Big" by David J. Schwartz.

Objective: To apply the five key lessons from the book to enhance your grant-seeking mindset and strategies.

Steps:

1. Believe in Your Vision:
- Take time to reflect on your organization's mission and vision. Ensure that your team genuinely believes in the importance of your work. Discuss the significance of your cause and the positive impact it can have on your community.

2. Set Ambitious Goals:
- Review your organization's grant goals and objectives. Are they ambitious enough? Consider setting new, higher targets that reflect the significant impact you aim to achieve with grant funding. Brainstorm with your team to identify grander goals.

3. Cultivate a Positive Attitude:
- Evaluate your attitude and the attitudes of your team members when it comes to grant-seeking. Encourage a positive and can-do spirit within your organization. Discuss your achievements and focus on maintaining an optimistic approach to challenges.

4. Take Decisive Action:
- Assess your grant-seeking strategies and processes. Identify areas where you can be more proactive and decisive. Develop an action plan that outlines specific steps for enhancing your grant acquisition efforts. Assign responsibilities within your team for each action item.

5. Learn from Setbacks:
- Acknowledge that setbacks and rejections are a part of the grant-seeking journey. Rather than being discouraged, view each setback as an opportunity for learning and improvement. Discuss how your organization can adapt its approach based on past experiences.

6. Create a Grant-Seeking Success Plan:
- Based on the five key lessons, create a Grant-Seeking Success Plan for your organization. This plan should outline your commitment to thinking big, setting ambitious goals, maintaining a positive attitude, taking decisive action, and learning from setbacks.

7. Regularly Review and Revise:
- Periodically revisit your Grant-Seeking Success Plan. Assess your progress and make necessary adjustments. Ensure that your organization remains aligned with the principles of thinking big.

8. Share the Vision:
- Ensure that your team members are aware of the plan and fully committed to its principles. Encourage regular meetings to discuss progress and share ideas for thinking big in your grant-seeking activities.

9. Apply the Lessons:
- Implement the five lessons and your Grant-Seeking Success Plan in your daily grant acquisition activities. Encourage your team to embody these principles in interactions with potential funders and partners.

10. Celebrate Achievements:
- Celebrate your grant-seeking achievements and milestones, regardless of their scale. Recognize the progress your organization has made and the positive impact you've had on your community.

By applying these "Thinking Big" principles to your grant-seeking process, you can enhance your organization's mindset and approach, increasing your potential to secure grants and make a more significant impact on the causes you support.

Think BIGGER!

Discussion Questions

1. The story highlights Mr. Grant Money's key lessons from "The Magic of Thinking Big" by David J. Schwartz and how they apply to grant acquisition. How can these lessons be adapted and implemented by organizations and individuals seeking grant funding? What practical steps can grant seekers take to believe in their vision, set ambitious goals, maintain a positive attitude, take decisive action, and learn from setbacks in their grant acquisition efforts?

2. Mr. Grant Money mentions that a positive attitude is vital throughout the grant-seeking process. How can this notion serve as a starting point for discussing the role of attitude and mindset in grant acquisition? What strategies or techniques can grant seekers use to cultivate and maintain a positive attitude, and how can it influence their interactions with funders and collaborators?

3. The Alamo, an iconic historical site, left Mr. Grant Money unimpressed. How can this observation prompt a discussion about the importance of context and perspective in grant acquisition? What factors might influence how grant seekers perceive or value their projects or objectives, and how can they align their work with the interests and priorities of potential funders?

4. The story humorously mentions Mr. Grant Money's gold notebook, which contains essential lessons for grant acquisition success. How can this element lead to a conversation about the importance of knowledge management and continuous learning in the grant field? What are some effective strategies for documenting, organizing, and applying lessons and insights from past grant acquisition experiences?

5. Mr. Grant Money reflects on his first grant success—a $400,000 grant for a client. How can this anecdote prompt a discussion about the significance of early successes and the impact they can have on an individual's or organization's grant acquisition journey? What can organizations and grant seekers learn from their early achievements, and how can these insights be applied to future grant-seeking efforts?

💡 Big Idea "The "Favor Bank" Networking App"

Capitalize on the idea of Mr. Grant Money's influential allies and the concept of favors owed. Create a networking app designed specifically for grant seekers and nonprofit professionals. The "Favor Bank" app would allow users to connect, exchange favors, and build relationships to enhance their chances of securing grants. Users could list their skills, assets, or connections and request or offer assistance in grant acquisition. This innovative approach could turn the art of networking into a strategic grant acquisition tool.

🔍 Word Search

Enter the world of Mr. Grant Money's adventures in the historic city of San Antonio, Texas. As he explores the Alamo and the enchanting Riverwalk, he reflects on the valuable lessons from a book that are essential for those seeking grant funding.

In this puzzle, discover the words related to the extraordinary adventures of Mr. Grant Money. Can you find all the hidden words that capture the essence of this remarkable story?

Now, here are the 15 words for the word search puzzle based on the story:

A	I	G	O	M	A	L	A	O	S	C	S	O	I
B	I	S	A	T	T	I	T	U	D	E	L	L	U
B	C	T	A	K	L	A	W	R	E	V	I	R	C
M	G	N	I	K	N	I	H	T	C	N	I	I	C
A	S	N	O	S	S	E	L	I	N	A	O	S	I
G	N	O	I	S	I	V	I	S	S	T	S	O	A
I	G	T	S	S	E	N	I	S	I	U	C	D	C
C	O	T	I	A	S	A	W	U	T	A	I	K	A
S	A	N	A	N	T	O	N	I	O	S	O	I	C
E	L	K	G	O	L	D	M	I	N	E	S	T	T
C	S	I	I	G	G	A	L	V	S	A	I	I	I
A	L	A	S	S	K	C	A	B	T	E	S	O	O
I	G	V	N	T	A	K	D	N	A	E	O	S	N
Y	E	L	K	R	A	B	S	E	L	R	A	H	C

CUISINE
LESSONS
BIG
VISION
ATTITUDE
ALAMO
RIVERWALK
MAGIC
GOLD-MINE
ACTION
GOALS
THINKING
CHARLES BARKLEY
SETBACKS
SAN ANTONIO

"Mr. Grant Money's time in San Antonio reminds us that inspiration can be found in the most unexpected places, and that each location can hold a unique meaning to individuals. His valuable lessons about thinking big, embracing positivity, and learning from setbacks show the timeless wisdom that can guide organizations in their grant-seeking endeavors."

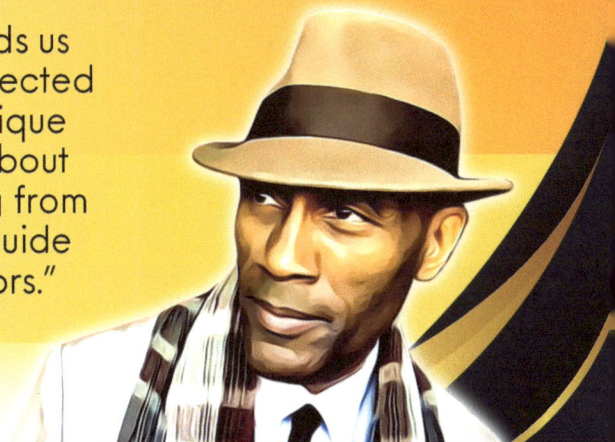

The Amazing Adventures of
MR GRANT MONEY

Grant Acquisition Unleashed: Mr. Grant Money's Art of Winning

From Denial to Victory – The $750,000 Kansas City Coup

In the vibrant heart of Kansas City, the always-dapper Mr. Grant Money, a true maestro of style who could give even the legendary Dapper Dan a run for his money, found himself engaged in a strategic consultation with a highly successful nonprofit organization. The mission at hand was to secure a coveted $750,000 grant from a large private foundation to fuel the development of a 10-agency partnership aimed at driving economic development in the city. This was no small task, especially considering that their request had been denied the previous year.

Mr. Grant Money approached this challenge like a master painter crafting a masterpiece, carefully selecting each brushstroke with precision and artistry. He knew that the key to success was not only in the final result but in the orchestration of every detail leading up to it.

One brilliant example of Mr. Grant Money's strategic genius was his creation of a comprehensive game plan that left no stone unturned. With the skill of an astute chess player, he positioned the nonprofit to be the shining star on a stage filled with contenders. He identified the weaknesses of the previous proposal and transformed them into strengths. He leveraged their unique assets and capabilities, crafting a narrative that was both compelling and irresistible.

But Mr. Grant Money's brilliance didn't stop at strategy; it extended to the art of relationship building. He knew that in the world of grants, personal connections could often tip the scales in one's favor. With a charisma that could charm the stars, he developed a personal communication strategy with key decision-making board members of the private foundation. Each interaction was carefully orchestrated, leaving a lasting impression of competence and dedication.

To further bolster the nonprofit's chances, Mr. Grant Money tapped into his highly guarded relationships with powerful individuals who owed him favors from past endeavors. These influential allies were more than happy to oblige his request, knowing that when Mr. Grant Money called, it was because he had a vision that was worth supporting.

As the final pieces of the puzzle fell into place, the nonprofit found themselves in a position of undeniable strength. They had transformed from an overlooked contender into the only viable option for funding the ambitious partnership.

When the grant was finally secured, Mr. Grant Money had a twinkle in his eye and a charming smile on his lips. It was a smile that said, "This was too easy," as he sped off in his sleek grey and black Porsche, the rooftop down, singing along with Frank Sinatra, "I did it my way."

In the world of grants, Mr. Grant Money's way was a path paved with brilliance, boldness, and a touch of magic that left a trail of success in his wake, one adventure at a time.

> "In the realm of grant acquisition, success doesn't come by chance; it's crafted with the precision of a master painter, each brushstroke a strategic move. Just like a painting, your proposal should be a masterpiece, capturing the hearts and minds of funders."
>
> -Mr. Grant Money

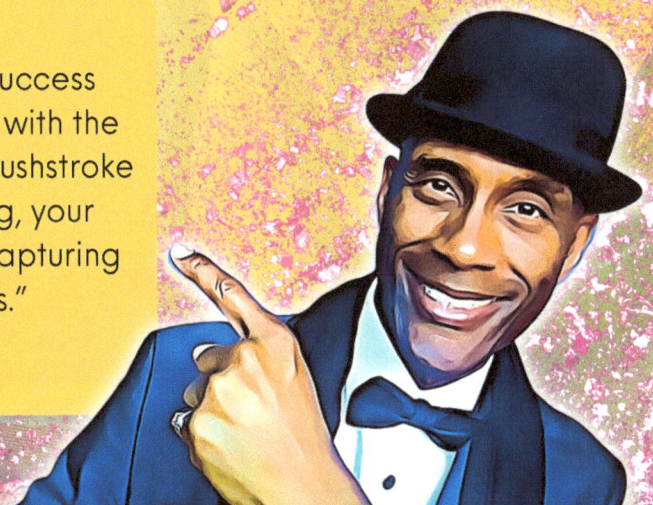

Exercise: "Strategic Grant Acquisition Makeover"

This exercise is designed to help individuals or organizations seeking grants take a strategic approach to enhance their grant acquisition efforts, inspired by Mr. Grant Money's tactics in the story.

Objective: To develop a strategic game plan for securing grants, focusing on turning past weaknesses into strengths, building relationships with key decision-makers, and leveraging influential allies to bolster your chances of success.

Steps:

1. Self-Assessment:
- Take a moment to reflect on your previous grant-seeking attempts or challenges. Identify weaknesses, areas for improvement, and aspects that have previously hindered your success. Be honest about past setbacks.

2. Strengths and Unique Assets:
- List your organization's unique strengths, assets, and capabilities that could be leveraged in your grant applications. Think about what sets you apart from other contenders and how you can showcase these strengths.

3. Strategic Game Plan:
- Craft a comprehensive game plan for your grant acquisition efforts. Consider the weaknesses you identified in step 1 and strategize on how to turn them into strengths. This plan should be detailed and leave no room for missed opportunities.

4. Relationship Building:
- Identify key decision-makers or influencers within the grant-making organizations you are targeting. Develop a personalized communication strategy for engaging with them. This strategy should aim to build strong, positive relationships with these individuals.

5. Leveraging Influential Allies:
- Think about your network and whether there are influential individuals or allies who can support your grant-seeking efforts. Reach out to them and discuss how they can contribute, whether through introductions, endorsements, or other means.

6. Proposal Enhancement:
- Review a past or current grant proposal and apply the insights from steps 2, 3, and 4. Make sure your proposal highlights your strengths and addresses previous weaknesses. Ensure it's compelling and aligned with the grantor's priorities.

7. Trial Communication:
- Practice your communication strategy by reaching out to a mentor, friend, or colleague. Share your proposal and engage in a role-play exercise where they act as a key decision-maker. Receive feedback on your approach.

8. Seek Feedback and Adjust:
- Share your enhanced proposal with peers or colleagues for feedback. Consider their input and make necessary adjustments to your proposal and strategy.

9. Implementation:
- Start implementing your enhanced strategy and reach out to grantors. Be diligent in your communications and follow-ups, adhering to the plan you've crafted.

10. Monitor Progress:
- Regularly monitor your progress, document interactions with grantors, and be prepared to adapt your strategy as necessary. Learn from each interaction, whether it results in success or a setback.

11. Reflect on Success and Setbacks:
- As you navigate the grant-seeking process, regularly reflect on your experiences. Acknowledge and celebrate your successes and view setbacks as opportunities for improvement. Update your strategy accordingly.

12. Documentation and Learning:
- Keep a record of your interactions, strategies, and outcomes in a dedicated "Grant Acquisition Success Journal." This journal will serve as a valuable resource for future grant-seeking endeavors.

By following this exercise and implementing a strategic game plan inspired by Mr. Grant Money's tactics, you can increase your organization's chances of securing grants and achieve greater success in the grant acquisition process.

Discussion Questions

1. Mr. Grant Money's success in securing a $750,000 grant for the nonprofit organization is depicted as a work of art. What specific strategies and tactics did he employ to turn their fortunes around, and how did he transform the weaknesses of the previous proposal into strengths?

2. The story emphasizes the importance of personal connections and relationships in the grant acquisition process. How did Mr. Grant Money use his charisma and relationships to build a compelling case for the nonprofit's grant request, and what can other grant seekers learn from this approach?

3. Mr. Grant Money's approach is described as brilliant and strategic. What role did strategic planning play in the nonprofit's victory, and what were the key elements of the game plan that helped them stand out among competitors?

4. The story portrays Mr. Grant Money as a charismatic and influential figure in the world of grant acquisition. What are some ethical considerations in the world of grant-seeking and grant-making, especially when it comes to leveraging personal relationships and influential allies to secure funding?

5. Mr. Grant Money's success in this story is remarkable, but it also leaves us with the impression that his approach might not work for everyone. What are the limitations and challenges in implementing a grant acquisition strategy like Mr. Grant Money's, and what alternative approaches could nonprofit organizations consider when seeking grants?

💡 **Big Idea** "The Artistic Philanthropy Charity Auction"

Combine the world of art and philanthropy by organizing an annual charity auction event. Renowned artists, both established and emerging, would create and donate artworks inspired by stories of individuals, like Mr. Grant Money, who've made significant contributions to the world of grants and philanthropy. The proceeds from the auction would be used to support nonprofit organizations and educational initiatives that focus on grant acquisition, ensuring that future generations have access to valuable resources and training.

🔍 Word Search

Step into the world of Mr. Grant Money's strategic brilliance and suave style in the vibrant heart of Kansas City. Explore the artistry of grant acquisition as you uncover the hidden words related to Mr. Grant Money's mission to secure a $750,000 grant for a nonprofit organization.

In this puzzle, discover the words related to the extraordinary adventures of Mr. Grant Money. Can you find all the hidden words that capture the essence of this remarkable story?

Now, here are the 15 words for the word search puzzle based on the story:

```
R E L A T I O N S H I P S A
E S G A M E P L A N N G C M
S S O D E V E L O P M E N T
T U C I M O N O C E C N N L
R C C O N S U L T A T I O N
A C P E P T A M E G L P M I
T E P L L C I C H O E D T P
E S E A O E H E G D F O E L
G S L P T A M A E S T R O C
I L Y N R D A P P E R D A N
C I T I E N O N P R O F I T
E A S O C H A L L E N G E P
I M I N F L U E N C E N O I
A N L A T N A N K A N S A S
```

NONPROFIT
CONSULTATION
KANSAS
SUCCESS
STRATEGIC
CHARISMA
GAME PLAN
ECONOMIC
INFLUENCE
CHALLENGE
DEVELOPMENT
MAESTRO
RELATIONSHIP
STYLE
DAPPER DAN

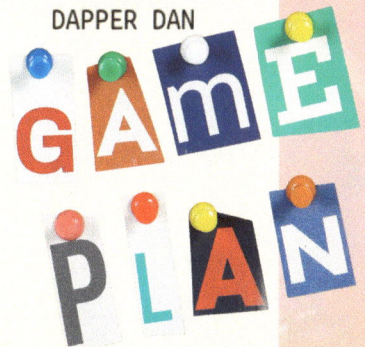

GAME PLAN

"The success story of Kansas City reminds us that with the right strategy, brilliance, and relationships, even the most challenging grant acquisition missions can be accomplished. It's a testament to the power of meticulous planning and the art of persuasion in the world of grants."

Brushstrokes of Wisdom: Mr. Grant Money's Artistic Adventure

*Grant Acquisition Lessons Painted in
Love and Creativity*

After leaving the luxurious shores of Trinidad, Mr. Grant Money boarded a plane bound for Dallas, Texas. It was a journey that held a special place in his heart, for it meant spending quality time with his family, including his father, Fred Walker, a man known for his impeccable style and business acumen, and his brother Chris.

As much as Mr. Grant Money was a demanding and high-performance individual in his professional life, he had a soft spot reserved for two little girls who held a special place in his heart—his nieces, Christina and Crystal. These two bright-eyed youngsters shared a deep love for art, a passion that Uncle Rod, as they affectionately called him, wholeheartedly embraced.

Once Mr. Grant Money transformed into Uncle Rod, all formalities were cast aside, and he dedicated himself to being the loving and doting uncle that Christina and Crystal adored. He cherished them as the gifts they were, especially since he saw traces of himself and his beloved mother in both of them.

One sunny afternoon, as they gathered around a table covered in colorful paints, brushes, and blank canvases, Uncle Rod engaged in a heartwarming conversation with his nieces.

"So, what magnificent works of art shall we create today, my talented artists?" he asked with a playful twinkle in his eye.

The girls beamed with excitement, each eager to embark on their artistic journey. As they dipped their brushes into vibrant colors and let their imaginations run wild, Mr. Grant Money reveled in the simple joy of being present in the moment.

As the afternoon unfolded, amidst laughter and the gentle swish of brushes on canvas, Mr. Grant Money shared a promise with Christina and Crystal. He told them that he would keep each of their precious works of art safely stored until they were adults, ready to show their own children the beauty of their childhood creativity.

Before they wrapped up their artistic adventure, Mr. Grant Money brought out his trusted gold notebook. It was a ritual he followed, like collecting the treasures of wisdom that life had to offer. He jotted down an important life lesson:

"Art, like grant acquisition, is a journey of creativity and persistence. Just as every brushstroke contributes to a masterpiece, every grant application adds to the canvas of change. The true beauty lies not only in the finished work but in the passion and dedication poured into it."

With these words of wisdom captured in his golden notebook, Mr. Grant Money felt a profound sense of fulfillment. It was a reminder that life's most cherished moments often lay in the simplest of joys and connections. As he looked at Christina and Crystal, he couldn't help but marvel at the boundless potential within them and the incredible journey of life they had ahead.

With a loving smile, Mr. Grant Money collected their artwork, knowing that these pieces would one day be a testament to the precious bond they shared. It was a bond that extended beyond family ties—it was a celebration of the beauty of art, the magic of family, and the power of love.

As he left Dallas and returned to his world of grants and acquisitions, Mr. Grant Money carried with him not only the artwork of his nieces but also the reminder that the truest treasures in life were the moments spent with loved ones, and the wisdom gathered along the way, each page of his gold notebook a testament to the valuable lessons he had learned and shared.

Exercise: "The Artistic Wisdom of Life and Grant Acquisition"

This exercise is designed to help individuals reflect on the connection between art, life, and grant acquisition and extract valuable insights from Mr. Grant Money's story.

Objective: To recognize the parallels between the art of creating, life experiences, and the grant acquisition process, and to appreciate the wisdom that can be drawn from these connections.

Steps:

1. Reflect on Your Own Passions:
- Take a moment to think about your own interests and passions outside of your professional life. Are there activities or hobbies you engage in that bring you joy, just as art does for Christina and Crystal? It could be anything creative, like painting, music, writing, or any other activity.

2. Identify Parallels with Grant Acquisition:
- Consider how the process of engaging in your passion or hobby parallels the grant acquisition process. Are there similarities in terms of dedication, creativity, and persistence? Think about how the principles you apply to your passion can be applied to securing grants.

3. Capture Personal Wisdom:
- In your own notebook or journal, jot down insights from these parallels. Reflect on how the joy and dedication you find in your passion can translate into your professional life, especially in the grant acquisition journey.

4. Share the Experience:
- If you have children, nieces, nephews, or younger family members, take a moment to engage with them in your chosen creative activity. Much like Uncle Rod, use this as an opportunity to bond with them and impart valuable lessons, just as he shared his wisdom with Christina and Crystal.

"Just as every brushstroke contributes to a masterpiece, each grant application adds to the canvas of change. It's not just the final result that matters, but the passion and dedication poured into the process that makes the difference."

–Mr. Grant Money

5. Capture the Moment:

- As you engage in creative activities with your young relatives or loved ones, take a picture or video to commemorate the moment. These memories can be a source of inspiration and can serve as a reminder of the importance of life beyond work.

6. Reflect on the Bigger Picture:

- Think about how the exercise of teaching and connecting with your loved ones through creativity reminds you of the bigger picture. This lesson can extend to your professional life, highlighting the importance of relationships, inspiration, and shared experiences.

7. Artistic Wisdom for Grant Acquisition:

- Consider the wisdom Mr. Grant Money shared in his golden notebook and how it applies to grant acquisition. Note how each step in the grant application process, much like a brushstroke, contributes to a larger canvas of change and impact.

8. Apply the Insight:

- Return to your work in grant acquisition with the insights gained. Apply the principles of dedication, creativity, and persistence to your grant proposals and strategies, with the understanding that the true beauty of the work lies in the passion and effort invested.

9. Keep an Artistic Wisdom Journal:

- Create a journal or notebook dedicated to capturing sights and lessons from both your creative passion and your professional life. Similar to Mr. Grant Money's gold notebook, this journal can serve as a source of wisdom and reflection.

By engaging in this exercise, you can recognize the interconnectedness of your passions, your personal life, and your professional journey. You'll gather valuable insights from your own experiences and Mr. Grant Money's story, combining artistic wisdom with the art of grant acquisition.

"In art and in grant acquisition, the true beauty lies in the journey, in the creativity and persistence. Remember, my young artists, your potential is as boundless as the imagination you pour onto your canvases."

-Mr. Grant Money

Discussion Questions

1. The story portrays a different, more personal side of Mr. Grant Money's life as "Uncle Rod." What can we learn from the contrast between his professional life as a grant acquisition expert and his personal life as a dedicated uncle? How does this reflect the importance of work-life balance?

2. Mr. Grant Money emphasizes the parallel between art and grant acquisition, noting that both are journeys of creativity and persistence. How do the elements of creativity and dedication apply to the world of grant acquisition, and what can grant seekers learn from the artistic process?

3. The story highlights the importance of capturing life lessons and wisdom in a golden notebook. What are some life lessons shared by Mr. Grant Money that could be applied to grant acquisition or other aspects of life and work? How can the act of preserving wisdom be valuable for individuals and organizations?

4. Mr. Grant Money's promise to keep his nieces' artwork until they are adults is a touching gesture. How does this act symbolize the importance of preserving and celebrating the creativity and accomplishments of the next generation? How can this concept be extended to mentorship and support for aspiring grant seekers?

5. The story emphasizes the simple joys, connections, and moments spent with loved ones as true treasures in life. How can this message be applied to the sometimes-demanding world of grant acquisition and nonprofit work, and what strategies can grant seekers use to maintain a healthy work-life balance?

💡 **Big Idea** "Grant Acquisition Cruise Retreat"

Inspired by Mr. Grant Money's Caribbean cruise experience, the concept of a "Grant Acquisition Cruise Retreat" could be developed. This retreat would offer a unique and luxurious opportunity for grant seekers, nonprofit leaders, and government officials to embark on a cruise focused on grant acquisition.

Passengers would learn from grant experts, including Mr. Grant Money himself, as they sail to exotic destinations. Workshops, seminars, and one-on-one consultations would be conducted on board, teaching participants the art of securing grants while enjoying the elegance and style of a luxury cruise. The "Grant Acquisition Cruise Retreat" would provide a unique blend of education, relaxation, and networking, creating a memorable and productive experience for attendees.

🔍 Word Search

Experience the heartwarming journey of Mr. Grant Money as he embraces the simple joys of life with his beloved family in Dallas, Texas. Dive into the world of love, art, and treasured moments shared with his nieces, Christina and Crystal. Discover the hidden words that reflect the wisdom, love, and joy that paint the canvas of Uncle Rod's life.

In this puzzle, discover the words related to the extraordinary adventures of Mr. Grant Money. Can you find all the hidden words that capture the essence of this remarkable story?

Now, here are the 15 words for the word search puzzle based on the story:

A	J	U	N	C	L	E	R	O	D	H	N	N	E
Y	O	L	E	S	S	O	N	S	C	E	N	I	U
T	U	T	T	L	D	Y	H	Y	E	I	J	O	Y
I	R	E	W	P	D	F	A	M	I	L	Y	U	O
V	N	C	H	I	L	D	H	O	O	D	R	O	B
I	E	U	I	R	M	O	M	E	N	T	S	E	O
T	Y	L	N	W	N	S	E	N	Y	N	R	O	N
A	N	S	D	I	O	O	T	Y	B	S	O	Y	D
E	E	E	L	S	E	N	T	U	O	N	D	O	S
R	E	S	E	D	T	C	D	M	Y	N	R	S	I
C	S	M	I	O	I	A	E	N	E	N	S	S	J
I	A	S	O	M	Y	O	R	S	S	T	C	E	R
T	R	E	A	S	U	R	E	T	J	O	T	E	I
O	N	L	O	V	E	S	I	M	O	R	P	O	P

Word list:
- BONDS
- PROMISE
- LESSONS
- MOMENTS
- WISDOM
- FAMILY
- JOURNEY
- NIECES
- CHILDHOOD
- JOY
- LOVE
- ART
- CREATIVITY
- UNCLE ROD
- TREASURE

"Mr. Grant Money's special bond with his nieces reminds us that amidst the demands of our high-performance lives, it's the simple joys and connections with loved ones that truly enrich our existence. The precious moments we share are the real treasures that enrich the pages of our life's story."

AFTERWARD

Dear Readers, as you conclude this second volume of Mr. Grant Money's exhilarating adventures, we hope you've enjoyed your journey through the captivating stories and valuable lessons that lie within these pages. The "Artful Navigator" series has taken you to astonishing places and unveiled essential insights to transform your approach to grant acquisition. But your adventure is far from over.

We encourage you to reflect on the lessons you've learned and the experiences you've shared with Mr. Grant Money. Each story has offered you unique, actionable strategies that can help you navigate the world of grants with style and precision. Now, it's time to put these valuable lessons into practice.

Just like Mr. Grant Money, it's your turn to spread your wings and soar to new heights in the grant acquisition world. You've learned from the best; now it's time to be the best. With your newfound knowledge and creative insights, you can approach grant writing with newfound confidence and a sense of purpose.

If you're hungry for more knowledge and expertise, remember that there are additional volumes of Mr. Grant Money's adventures waiting for you. Continue the journey through Volume 3 and beyond, where new stories and lessons await. Embrace these volumes as opportunities to explore fresh insights, discover innovative strategies, and evolve as a grant acquisition expert.

Beyond the books, Mr. Grant Money offers further resources and assistance through Grant Central USA and GrantAcquisition.com. Explore the in-depth training sessions to enhance your grant-writing skills and gain a deeper understanding of the grant acquisition process. Whether you're a seasoned grant professional or a newcomer, there's always room to grow and excel in this dynamic field.

Additionally, if you wish to embody Mr. Grant Money's style and elegance in your grant acquisition journey, visit GrantWriterStore.com. Here, you'll find a range of apparel that can help you look the part as you confidently navigate the world of grants.

As you embark on the next phase of your grant acquisition adventure, remember this powerful thought:

"Success is not final, failure is not fatal: It is the courage to continue that counts." – Winston Churchill

The journey you're on is a continuous one, filled with twists, turns, and valuable lessons. Embrace it with unwavering determination, just as Mr. Grant Money does in every one of his exciting adventures. The grant acquisition world is yours to conquer, and the adventures ahead will provide endless opportunities to soar to new heights.

ABOUT THE AUTHOR

Rodney Walker is a man on a mission. He's dedicated his life to helping others secure funding for their projects and dreams. As the President of Grant Central USA, a grant development training firm internationally known for helping organizations land six-figure and seven-figure grants and shave months off the time it takes to get funded, Rodney has helped clients raise over half a billion dollars in grants!

He's also an author of numerous books, online courses and the founder of two popular grant writing conferences: The Education Grants Conference and First Responders Grants Conference. Grant Central USA has also partnered with several universities, including Regis University, Hawaii University, Oklahoma University, National University, Cal Poly University, and Florida Atlantic University.

Rodney is even the host of four podcasts: Get Funded with Rodney, Grant Writing Today, Grant Business Show, and Schools Winning Grants. He oversees Grant Success Advisors, an elite network of approved licensees who deliver today's leading training in grant development systems.

He has an extensive network of high-level contacts, including his Grant Writers Association group on Linkedin with over 15,000+ members.

Considered a national authority in the grant industry, Grant Central USA's clients have included, The Magic Johnson Foundation, the George W. Bush Foundation, Ben Guillory and Danny Glover of the Robey Theatre Company, Hawaii State Teachers Association, United Way, Habitat for Humanity, and numerous school districts and city governments.

Rodney has produced over 730 videos on grant development on his popular YouTube channel and has taught over 240,000 people how to improve their grant writing efforts. "We have been helping our clients successfully get funded and launch new careers in grant writing since 2006 across the U.S. and worldwide, giving them both the competence and the confidence to win the grants at a high level."

He says his primary specialty is "Getting our clients funded with six-figure and seven-figure grants while helping grant professionals get paid what they are worth!"

In addition to his leadership experience at Grant Central USA, he has years of experience in Business and Professional Development in various sectors. He has been a sought-after expert in grant professional development, coaching, and the law of success.

As a media personality, he has interviewed numerous celebrities, including Snoop Dogg, Heisman Trophy Winners: Reggie Bush, Charles Woodson, Professional Boxer Laila Ali, America's Next Top Model Season 19 Winner: Laura James, NBA Champions: Draymond Green, Matt Barnes, National College Football Champions: Coach Mack Brown, and Vince Young, and countless others.

It's safe to say that Rodney knows his stuff regarding grants and working with champions!

GRANT MONEY MAGNET™

I am the Grant Money Magnet™, a relentless force that navigates the intricate maze of grant acquisition with unwavering determination and a strategic mind. Challenges are not obstacles; they are opportunities waiting to be seized. With every hurdle, I rise, armed with innovative solutions, pushing the boundaries of what's possible. My curiosity is my compass, guiding me through the maze of grant landscapes, uncovering hidden opportunities and transforming challenges into triumphs.

In the realm of grant development campaigns, I am the orchestrator of a symphony that goes beyond the basics of mere grant writing. My daily actions are a testament to my commitment, with well-defined grant goals propelling me forward. I am not a lone warrior; I am part of a powerful grant team, where collaboration amplifies our impact. Together, we transcend the ordinary, transforming aspirations into tangible results.

Grant funding doesn't elude me; I attract it with an irresistible magnetic force. My mind is a powerhouse of ideas, a generator of solutions that resonate with the aspirations of benefactors and the needs of society. Relentlessness is my mantra; there's no door I can't open, no avenue left unexplored. I don't just pursue grants; I nurture relationships, cultivating a network of allies who share my passion for impact. In my grant pursuit, I don't just raise funds; I raise friends and partners, forging alliances that extend beyond transactions into enduring collaborations.

As the architect of my grant destiny, I recognize that true power lies not just in acquiring funds but in the collective strength of a united effort. I am not merely a seeker of grants; I am a catalyst for transformative change. With each campaign, I etch my mark on the maze of philanthropy, weaving a narrative of impact that transcends the ordinary. Together with my grant team, I shape a future where challenges bow before innovation, and the resonance of our collaborative endeavors echoes through the corridors of progress. Grant by grant, we sculpt a legacy that stands as a testament to the limitless potential of unified action and unwavering dedication.

Recite and embrace the power of this statement daily; let its resonance shape your mindset and fuel your unwavering commitment to grant success.

GRANTOPOLY ROYAL RULES

Dive into a realm of funding mastery with Mr. Grant Money's 10 Grantopoly Royal Rules For Engagement - your strategic guide to securing maximum funding for your organization. Revisit these rules often and witness your grant success soar as you put them into practice! 🚀💲 #GrantMastery #FundingSuccess

1. 🎯 **Master the Mission:** Clearly articulate your organization's mission in every proposal, demonstrating an unwavering commitment to your cause.

2. ☀️ **Impact is King:** Highlight the tangible, life-changing impact of your projects; grantors want to see real results.

3. 🤝 **Build Strategic Alliances:** Showcase partnerships with other organizations to demonstrate a united front in achieving common goals.

4. 📊 **Data Speaks Louder:** Back your proposals with compelling data and statistics that underscore the urgency and necessity of your work.

5. 📖 **Storytelling Magic:** Craft narratives that evoke empathy, connecting the funder emotionally to your mission and beneficiaries.

6. 💲 **Budget Brilliance:** Develop meticulously detailed budgets that align with project goals and ensure every dollar is well-spent.

7. 📈 **Transparent Metrics:** Articulate clear and measurable outcomes, outlining how the funding will drive positive change.

8. 🌐 **Engage the Community:** Illustrate strong community involvement and support, reflecting a broad network invested in your success.

9. 🔄 **Continuous Learning:** Demonstrate a commitment to improvement through feedback loops and adaptive strategies.

10. 🙏 **Express Gratitude:** Always express sincere gratitude for the grantor's consideration, building a foundation for long-term partnerships.

MR. GRANT MONEY'S IDIOMS

Welcome to a world of financial creativity and linguistic flair! In this collection, you'll find ten unique "Mr. Grant Money" idioms crafted to add a touch of wit and imagination to your discussions about grants and funding opportunities. These idioms are not just expressions; they're windows into the dynamic and often challenging realm of grant acquisition. Enjoy more of these with new ones in the next volumes.

1. **Riding the Grant Wave:**
Meaning: Benefiting from a surge in available grant opportunities or a favorable funding environment.

2. **Grants in the Pipeline:**
Meaning: Anticipating and preparing for upcoming grant opportunities.

3. **A Penny for Your Grant Thoughts:**
Meaning: Encouraging someone to share their ideas and strategies for securing grants.

4. **Grant Hurdles and Hoops:**
Meaning: Navigating through challenges and obstacles in the grant application and approval process.

5. **Casting the Grant Net Wide:**
Meaning: Applying for grants from various sources to increase the chances of securing funding.

6. **Granting the Midas Touch:**
Meaning: Having the ability to turn grant funds into successful and impactful projects.

7. **The Grant Maze:**
Meaning: Facing a complex and confusing process when navigating grant regulations and requirements.

8. **Counting Grant Stars:**
Meaning: Feeling optimistic about the potential success of a grant application or project.

9. **Granting a Silver Lining:**
Meaning: Finding positive aspects or opportunities within a challenging or competitive grant environment.

10. **The Grant Phoenix:**
Meaning: Rising from setbacks or failures in grant applications to achieve success in subsequent attempts.

INFORMATIONAL INTERVIEW

Informational interviews are an excellent way to gain valuable insights and knowledge from experienced grant professionals and grant makers. By engaging in conversations with experts in the field, you can enhance your understanding, learn best practices, and foster your continuous growth and development in the world of grant funding.

Instructions:

1. **Identify Potential Interviewees:**
   - Create a list of grant professionals, grant makers, and other individuals with relevant insights whom you would like to interview. Consider factors such as expertise, experience, and industry focus.

2. **Reach Out:**
   - Craft a polite and concise email introducing yourself and explaining your interest in an informational interview. Request a convenient time for a meeting, either in person, over the phone, or via video call.

3. **Prepare Questions:**
   - Develop a list of thoughtful questions to guide your conversation. Tailor these questions to the individual's expertise and experiences. Be sure to ask about challenges they've faced, successes they've had, and advice they can offer.

4. **Schedule the Interview:**
   - Once you receive a positive response, schedule a time for the informational interview. Be respectful of their time and come prepared with your questions.

5. **Conduct the Interview:**
   - During the interview, actively listen, take notes, and ask follow-up questions. Be respectful of their time constraints and focus on extracting valuable insights.

6. **Reflect and Analyze:**
   - After each interview, take some time to reflect on the key takeaways. Consider how the information can be applied to your own work and goals.

7. **Thank You Note:**
   - Send a thank-you email expressing your gratitude for their time and insights. Mention specific points from the interview that were particularly helpful.

INFORMATIONAL INTERVIEW

Interviewee Information:

Name:
Title:
Organization:
Contact Information:
Date of Interview:

Interview Questions:

1. What led you to pursue a career in grant writing /management/grant making?
2. Can you share a significant challenge you faced in your career and how you overcame it?
3. What are the key skills and qualities you believe are crucial for success in this field?
4. How do you stay updated on the latest trends and changes in the grant industry?
5. Can you provide insights into your most successful grant project? What made it successful?
6. What advice do you have for someone looking to advance their career in grant management/grant making?
7. Are there any common misconceptions about working in grant-related roles that you'd like to address?

Key Takeaways:

Learnings:
Actionable Steps:
Connections Made:

Next Steps:

Identify Additional Contacts:
Schedule Next Informational Interview:
Implement Insights into Your Work:

This worksheet is designed to guide you through the process of conducting informational interviews and extracting valuable information to support your continuous growth and development in the field of grant funding. Good luck!

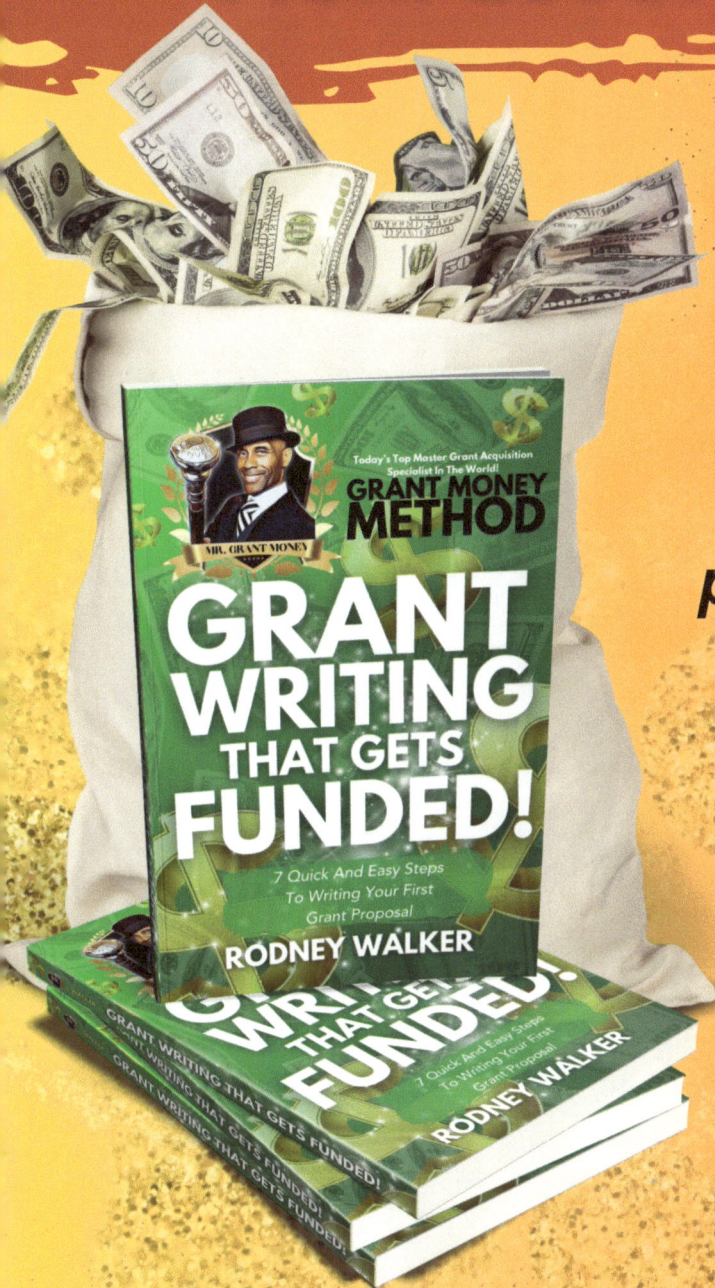

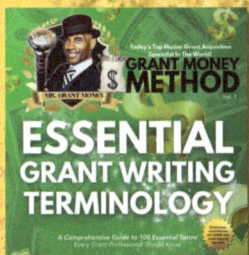

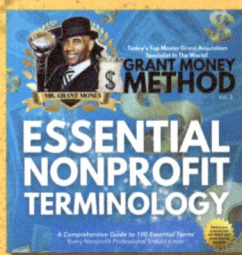

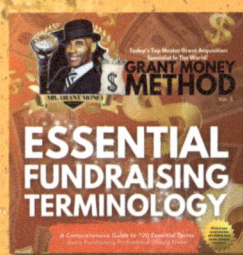

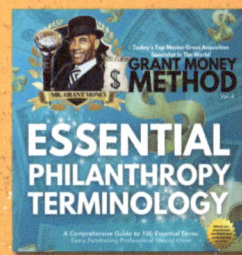

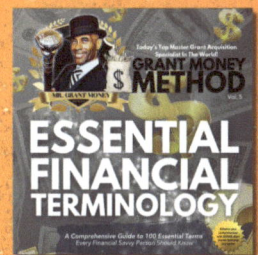

MGM Music to Get You Going 🎷 and 🎶 Keep You Soaring!

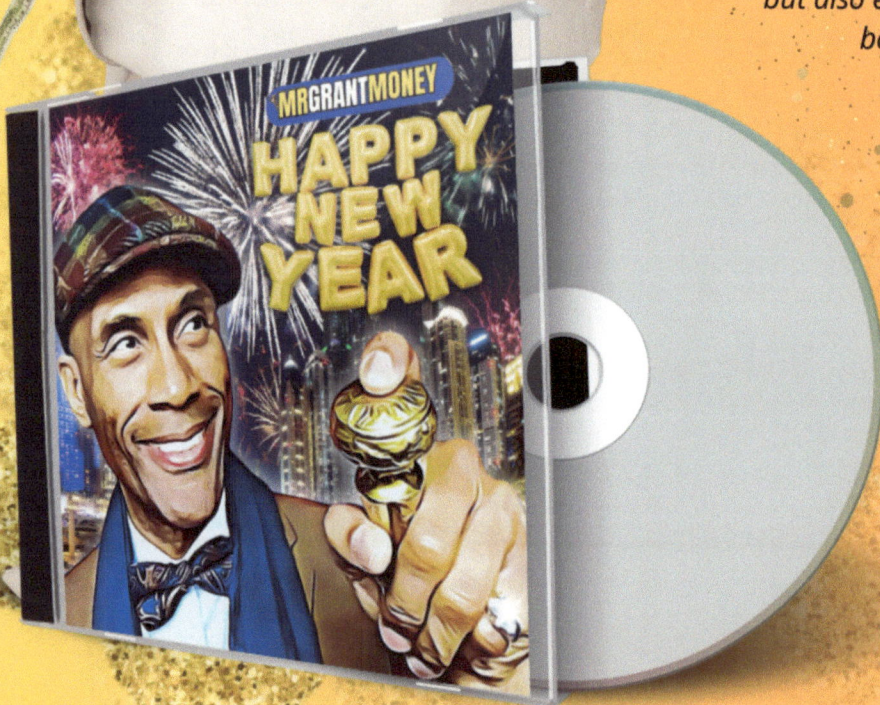

Music has the power to make life and learning more joyful. Get ready to have a blast with Mr. Grant Money Music, where every tune is fun, upbeat, and filled with positivity. These story-driven songs not only entertain but also educate and inspire, making your journey both enjoyable and enriching. 🎶

Dive into a symphony of stories and inspiration with Mr. Grant Money Music, where every note is a step toward greater success.

You can enjoy Mr. Grant Money Music on most major streaming platforms, including Spotify, Apple Music, and Amazon Music, bringing inspiration and positivity right to your favorite device. 🎧

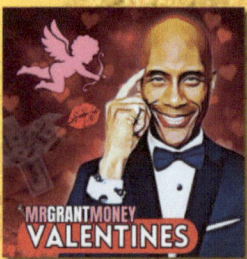

Diverse Musical Flavors to Satisfy Every Listening Craving

Topical and Seasonal Themes

Enjoy our themed musical sessions that align with the seasons and current events, offering fresh perspectives and innovative ideas from today's Top Master Grant Acquisition Specialist, Mr. Grant Money!

Experience Our Other Dynamic Series with Mr. Grant Money!

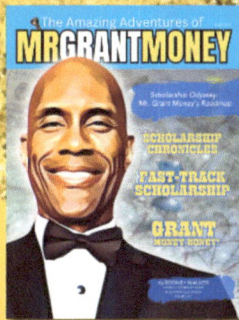

Scholarship Odyssey: Mr. Grant Money's Roadmap

Vol. 1

ISBN 979-8-89725-000-4

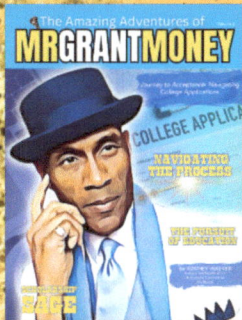

Journey To Acceptance: Navigating College Applications

Vol. 2

ISBN 979-8-89725-001-1

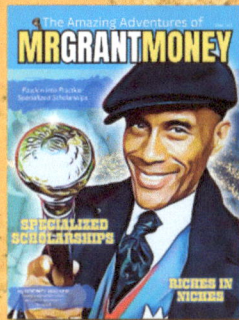

Passion Into Practice: Specialized Scholarship

Vol. 3

ISBN 979-8-89725-002-8

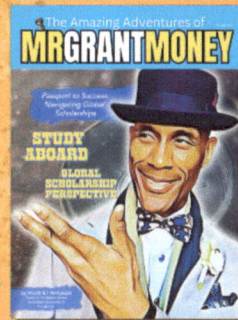

Passport To Success: Navigating Global Scholarships

Vol. 4

ISBN 979-8-89725-003-5

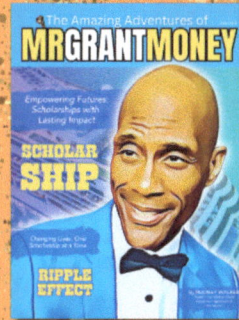

Empowering Futures: Scholarships With Lasting Impact

Vol. 5

ISBN 979-8-89725-004-2

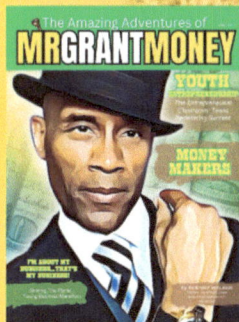

The Entrepreneurial Classroom: Teens Redefining Success

Vol. 1

ISBN 979-8-89725-005-9

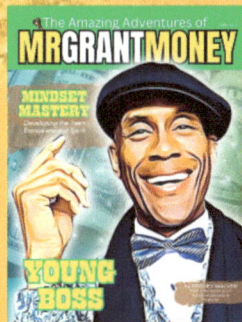

Mindset Mastery: Developing The Teen Entrepreneurial Spirit

Vol. 2

ISBN 979-8-89725-006-6

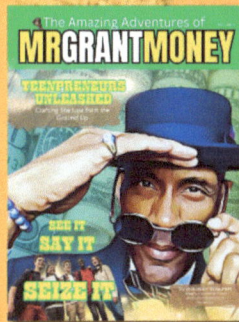

Teenpreneurs Unleashed: Crafting Startups From The Ground Up

Vol. 3

ISBN 979-8-89725-007-3

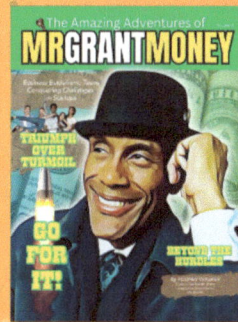

Business Battlefront: Teens Conquering Challenges In Startups

Vol. 4

ISBN 979-8-89725-008-0

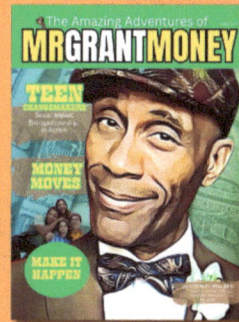

Teen Changemakers: Social Impact Entrepreneurship in Action

Vol. 5

ISBN 979-8-89725-009-7

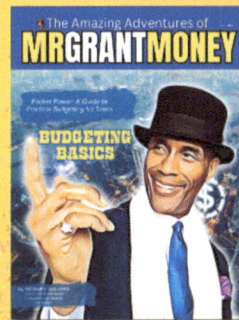

Pocket Power: A Guide to Practical Budgeting for Teens

Vol. 1

ISBN 979-8-89725-010-3

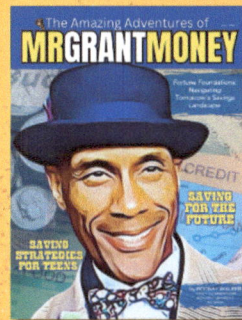

Fortune Foundations: Navigating Tomorrow's Savings Landscape

Vol. 2

ISBN 979-8-89725-011-0

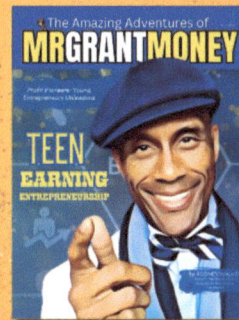

Profit Pioneers: Young Entrepreneurs Unleashed

Vol. 3

ISBN 979-8-89725-012-7

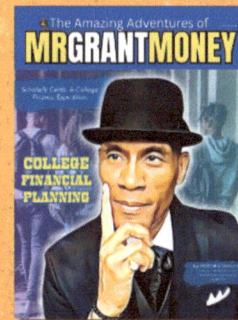

Scholarly Cents: A College Finance Expedition

Vol. 4

ISBN 979-8-89725-013-4

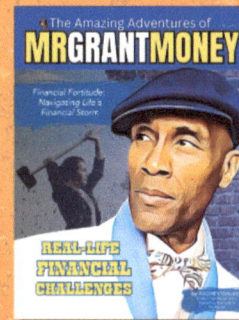

Financial Fortitude: Navigating Life's Financial Storm

Vol. 5

ISBN 979-8-89725-014-1

Enjoy More Amazing Adventures with Mr. Grant Money!

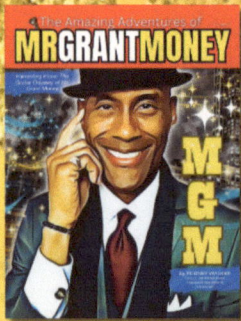

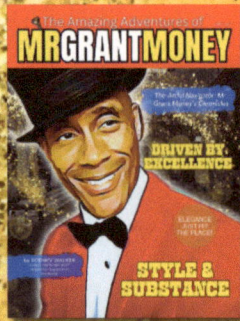

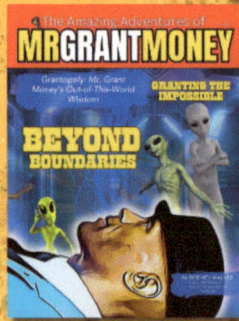

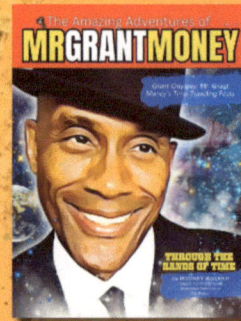

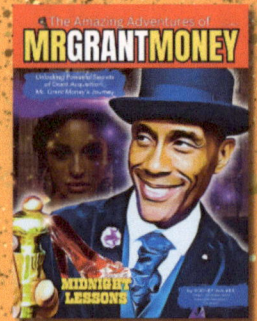

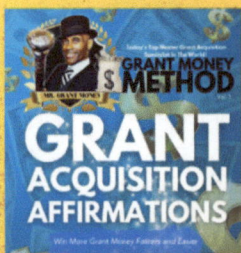

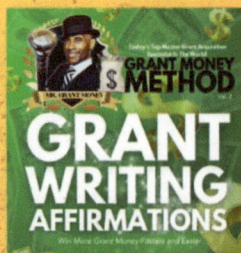

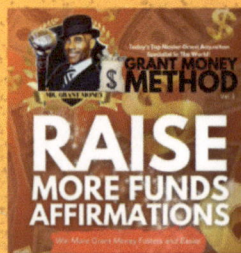

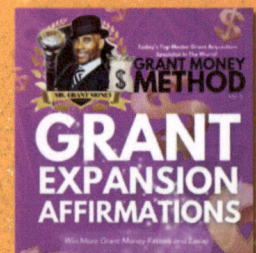

www.ingramcontent.com/pod-product-compliance
Lightning Source LLC
Chambersburg PA
CBHW041449210326
41599CB00004B/194